DOING BUSINESS ON

NEW TECHNOLOGY

DOING BUSINESS ON THE INTERNET

How to use the new technology
to win a competitive edge

Graham Jones

How To Books

Cartoons by Mike Flanagan

British Library Cataloguing in Publication Data
A catalogue record for this book is available from the British Library.

First published in 1997 by How To Books Ltd, Plymbridge House,
Estover Road, Plymouth PL6 7PZ, United Kingdom. Tel: Plymouth
(01752) 202301. Fax: (01752) 202331.

Note: The material contained in this book is set out in good faith for
general guidance and no liability can be accepted for loss or expense
incurred as a result of relying in particular circumstances on statements
made in this book. The laws and regulations may be complex and liable to
change, and readers should check the current position with the relevant
authorities before making personal arrangements.

A number of trade names and trade marks are mentioned in this book. The author
and publisher acknowledge them as being the property of their respective owners.

The case studies in this book are fictional. Any resemblance to real people and
businesses is entirely co-incidental.

Produced for How To Books by Deer Park Productions.

Typeset by Concept Communications (Design & Print) Ltd, Crayford, Kent.
Printed and bound by Cromwell Press, Broughton Gifford, Melksham, Wiltshire.

Contents

List of Illustrations

Preface

This book is for anyone in business who wants to know more about the Internet and how this unique communications system can help. This book will not tell you in graphic detail how to connect to the Internet, how to use the software programs that help you look around the Internet, nor how to do all sorts of wizardry that Internet fans love doing. There are plenty of books around, including my own, *How to Use the Internet*, that provide that kind of information. Instead, this book is about the relationship between business and the Internet. It explains how businesses can exploit the Net and gain new customers and new ways of communicating. This book will tell you how to improve internal communications and highlight ways of collecting cash from around the world.

You will discover that this book also emphasises the international nature of the Internet. Your business on the Net will be open to anyone, around the globe. That often means new ways of thinking about your business and new ways of conducting transactions. Hence this book helps you consider the international nature of Internet business activities, prompts you to think positively about how your company could benefit, and explains what you need to consider to exploit the system fully.

Graham Jones
gjones@zoo.co.uk

1
Helping Your Business with the Internet

If you start – or have already started – to use the Internet to help your business, you will notice how rapidly things change. Indeed it is easy to forget that only in 1994 the Internet was not really much of a business tool and few companies even took it seriously. Now, the Internet has been hijacked by big businesses around the world and many of its the original uses are now marginalised. The Internet is now a very serious business tool that almost all businesses will benefit from. It has also developed new, revolutionary businesses and ways of working.

The Microsoft example

You need no more confirmation of this than to understand the situation of Microsoft. If you have lived outside the world of computers, you may not have heard of Microsoft. This is the company started by Bill Gates, now one of the world's richest men thanks to the immense success of Microsoft. His company is the world leader in software development and there is hardly a personal computer in the world that doesn't have some Microsoft product on it.

The company became increasingly successful and profitable by developing complete integrated packages of programs that could do everything you wanted, from writing a letter to organising a complete data retrieval system and doing the company accounts. This concept was 'Microsoft Office' and now many other competing companies have 'office' products.

Then Microsoft turned its attention to **Windows 95**, a system that allows you to use your computer with much greater ease. This system was launched simultaneously around the world in the early part of 1995. Millions upon millions of copies have been sold.

While Microsoft was busy developing and improving Office and Windows 95, the Internet was growing by leaps and bounds. The success of the Internet actually caught Microsoft napping. So much attention was being given to Office and Windows 95 that other companies, notably one named Netscape, were able to creep up on Microsoft and achieve domination.

11

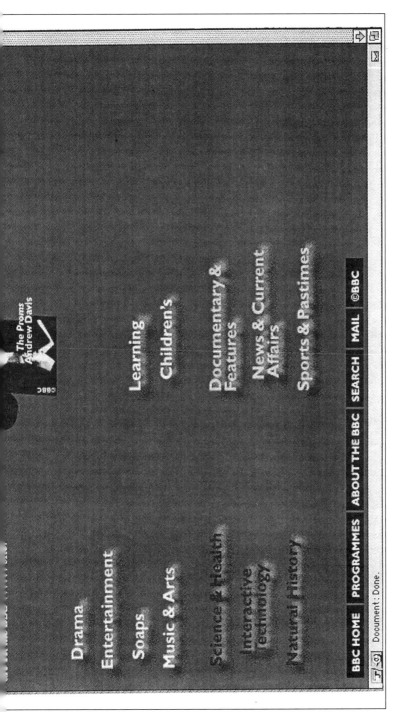

Fig. 1. Every kind of organisation is on the Internet: wherever you are in the world you can keep up to date with BBC programmes.

It is widely reported that Bill Gates realised he needed to do something drastic. His reputed knowledge of corporate histories showed him that firms that dillied and dallied suffered. Only by decisive action would Microsoft maintain its leadership position.

From a company that only had a minority interest in the Internet, Microsoft was transformed, almost overnight, into a company virtually centred on the Internet, The Internet is so important now that even the world's leading software company, Microsoft, needed to radically re-write its business plan and change direction dramatically.

Understanding the importance of the Internet

Microsoft has learned what many people in small business already knew. The Internet is a dramatic change in the way business is being done. Pundits predict that businesses that do not use the Internet in one way or another by the year 2000 won't be around by the year 2001. It is that important a development.

So Bill Gates is determined that the Internet will help his business. But what about yours? Have you planned a radical re-think, along the lines of Microsoft? Or are you just thinking about using the Internet? Time is running short and it will be easy for you to get left behind in the race towards the new way of business, unless you act quickly and decisively.

THINKING ABOUT YOUR BUSINESS

Before you can make any progress with the Internet, you need to do some clear thinking. You need to analyse your current position, consider where you want to be in two to three years' time and then think about how you might be able to get there. During this analysis you will find out whether or not the Internet can help you – if it can't you will be in a very rare kind of business!

Defining your business

Before you go any further obtain a clear picture of your current business. Write down the following items:

● name of business

● type of business

● legal entity (sole trader, partnership, private limited company, public limited company)

- years in business

- number of employees
  - now
  - at the start of your business

- number of customers
  - now
  - at the start of your business

- turnover for each of the last five years

- profit for each of the last five years

- company mission statement. If you don't have a mission statement write one now. Write up to 50 words which explain in detail the key reason for the existence of your business – what it does, how it will achieve it *etc.* For examples of mission statements read *The Seven Habits of Highly Effective People,* Stephen R Covey (Simon and Schuster Ltd, 1992).

These items will give you a written picture of your business (or of your department if you are in a large company). Now that you know where you are, you need to know where you are going. The key document that will help you with this is your **business plan**. Every business – from the smallest trader right through to the biggest multinational – should have a written business plan. If you don't have one, get writing now! (A complete guide to writing business plans appears in my book, *How to start a Business From Home.)*

Knowing where you want to go
Read through your business plan and note down the following key items:

any changes in the mission statement   _____

projected turnover for next two years   _____

projected profit for next two years   _____

projected customer base for next two years _____

key products/services being sold over
next two years _____

overall aim of business over next two years._____

These items will give you a picture of where you want to go. Now
compare it with the previous list of items that showed you where you are
now. By comparing the two, you can start to think about the journey you
might make from where you are now to your ultimate destination in a
couple of years' time.

Whether or not the Internet will be of any use to you during this journey will depend upon a variety of factors, too many to go into detail in
a short book. However, if any of the following factors occur during your
initial analysis, you business is almost certain to benefit from using the
Internet:

● desire to improve internal communications

● desire to improve external communications

● need to establish an international sales presence

● need to market products/services more widely

● desire to improve knowledge about competitors

● need to keep up to date with relevant information

● need to transmit important documents quickly and cheaply across
   the world

● desire to be seen as using the latest technology.

If any of these reasons occur to you during your analysis of your business journey over the next two years, you will benefit from using the
Internet. Even if none of these factors occurs during your initial planning, the Internet will still be likely to help. In preparing this book I went
through a host of business types to try and find one that definitely would
not benefit from using the Internet in one way or another. After weeks
of trying, I gave up!

Seeing the Internet strategically

However, the initial thinking process you have just done is important. Rather than see the Internet as something you just add on to your current business, you should now be able to begin to see the Internet in a strategic sense. The Internet should not be something you just add on to your current activities; instead, make the Internet a strategic part of your business and you will gain considerably more benefits.

FINDING OUT MORE ABOUT THE INTERNET

During your analysis of your business, you may have thought about such things as the need to improve **communications**. For example, your current business position may be one where profits are comparatively low because large expenses are incurred in communications with staff. To increase profits you need to reduce such costs. Therefore to get where you want to be in two years' time – higher profits – you need to increase the effectiveness of staff communications.

During your consideration of this topic it might not have occurred to you that the Internet is one way in which your costs can be reduced, your efficiency improved and your profits increased. So, before you finally decide whether or not to use the Internet in your business, find out some more about the Internet itself.

Sources of information

Naturally, reading this book will help. You should also read my previous book, *How to Use the Internet* (How To Books, 1996). Another good source of information is magazines on the Internet. The key ones to look out for are:

- *net*
- *The Internet*
- *NetUser.*

Don't be put off by the technical articles. Simply read the sections that show what kind of people are already on the Internet and the kinds of things they are doing. This should give you some idea of what is possible.

Visiting Internet cafés

Another way of finding out what is available on the Internet is to visit a specialist café. A leading chain is the 'Cybercafé'. These are cafeterias which also have computers linked to the Internet. One of the café staff will be happy to help you find out more about the Internet over a cup of coffee.

Some bookshops now also offer a similar service, where a corner of the shop is given over to an Internet area. Books on the Internet are available for purchase and there are computers linked to the Internet, with specialist shop staff available to help you find your way around, or simply tell you more.

So, find out as much as you can about the Internet and you will begin to see the opportunities. But will it really help your business?

DOING BUSINESS ON THE INTERNET

A quick scan of the Internet magazines will show you the enormous variety of ways in which businesses are exploiting the Internet. Many business are using the Internet as a means of communication; because you link to the Internet using a telephone call, you can contact staff and customers around the globe much more cheaply than ever before. Also, because you don't have to make calls at ridiculous hours due to time differences, it is also more convenient.

Many businesses are selling products and services over the Internet. You will find a whole host of products for sale from art and antiques to stocks and shares to venison, wine and zinc supplements! Lawyers do business over the Internet, as do writers, financial advisers and business consultants. So it's not just products, but services too that can be sold over the Internet.

Using the Internet for marketing

Some companies are not actually selling items over the Internet. Instead, they are using the facilities of the Internet to market their products and services, directing you to local sales outlets. Car manufacturers, for instance, are using the Internet to market their latest models. You can view the car from all angles, even see a video of it in action. You can look under the bonnet, see inside, read the technical specification – anything!

Other companies are also exploiting the Internet as a means of marketing their wares. They have their full, up to date, catalogue on line, for example. This means you get the latest information often more cheaply than driving to the local shop, paying to park and then finding the catalogue is out of date!

Gathering information

Some companies do not have an Internet presence of their own. Instead, they use the Internet to buy materials from suppliers or find out information from those already on the Internet. Say you were due to go on a business trip to Singapore. Finding out the latest information is easy using the Internet. Singapore has a significant amount of information of real use to the business traveller. Once you have read this, or saved it for future reading, you can then buy your airline ticket from an on-line travel agency. Now you can see whey many businesses are using the Internet for information retrieval and gaining supplies. The whole process can be integrated.

For instance, say you wanted to buy some specialist stationery. You could find out all about the product from independent information providers and then buy the materials from an on-line supplier. In the past you would need to visit a range of stationers, take their information with a pinch of salt as it would inevitably be biased and then return to the stationer of your choice. Now it can all be done with a single phone call and at local rates.

CHECKLIST

1. Before you start any kind of business activity on the Internet, plan how you will use this new technology. Don't integrate it within your business until you have discovered how it will help you achieve your goals.

2. Find out as much as you can about the Internet from a wide variety of sources before you dive in.

3. Don't forget, you don't have to have a presence on the Internet to get business value from it.

CASE STUDIES

Doing accounts over the Internet

Bryan is a freelance book-keeper. He is keen to widen his list of clients and is particularly keen to work via the Internet. His idea is that customers will send him their business accounts details via electronic mail. He can then prepare their accounts in a computerised accounts program and send them their completed books by electronic mail. This way customers will get their book-keeping done faster. He also believes it would be attractive to those customers who want to see their suppliers use the latest technology.

Bryan realises that the service he offers is little more than what is already done by other book-keepers, but he is sure that it will give him a competitive edge, particularly amongst the high tech companies who require book-keeping services. It will mark him out from the competition. Without the Internet he would need to work much harder to attract his key customers.

Running a Far East information service

Kim is a Malaysian business consultant who wants to increase his services to Europe. His concept is that businesses in Europe will want to know more about Malaysia and its business environment because of the rapid growth in the Asian economies. So Kim has set up an Internet presence. His information service provides up to date material on business activities in Malaysia and also gives Europeans a guide to business practices in the area. Additional services, such as specific searches for information, can be bought for a fee.

Kim charges a standard fee for each day's work – all explained on the Internet – and companies from Europe can order a specific number of days' consultancy. Kim then does the research they want, and sends his report via electronic mail to the client company. Without the Internet, Kim's business might not even exist because European businesses could not afford to wait for the information.

DISCUSSION POINTS

1. In what ways will the Internet help your business?

2. How might your business be radically transformed by the Internet?

3. What impact is the Internet likely to have on the business community you deal with regularly?

2
Getting Connected

To get connected to the Internet you need two key items:

- physical equipment

- an access account.

There are four key pieces of equipment that you need:

1. A computer.

2. A modem (device that connects your computer to a telephone line).

3. A telephone socket.

4. A printer (not vital but almost!).

CHOOSING YOUR EQUIPMENT

If you haven't already got computer equipment you will need to choose an Internet machine with care. Computers come in a variety of formats to reach as many potential markets as possible, so not every computer is ideal for Internet access. Getting access to the Internet means you need a fairly highly specified machine. Even though you can access the Internet with any computer – IBM PC, Macintosh, Amiga *etc* – you will need to ensure that whatever machine you use, it has the following characteristics:

- high speed

- plenty of memory

- plenty of storage space

- a relatively large, high speed, colour screen

- fast video

- multimedia capabilities

- a fast serial port.

In addition, your modem should:

- have high speed capabilities

- offer error correction.

Going for speed

As you can see, these lists can be summed up by saying that your computer and modem should be the **fastest** you can get. The faster your computer in every respect, the lower your charges for using the Internet. Naturally, your budget will play an important part in your decision making. But if just one part of your Internet usage is slowed down in any way, up goes your phone bill. So go for speed. The fastest machine you can afford will save you considerable amounts in the long term. In other words, don't let higher costs at the beginning put you off. It will save you a great deal of long term expenditure.

Upgrading your equipment

Many businesses, of course, will already have computers. Buying a new machine just for the Internet may not be justified. In this instance you should make sure that any machine you intend to use for Internet access is upgraded so that it matches the specification of a fast, new machine. The upgrades you should consider are:

- extra Random Access Memory (RAM)

- extra storage memory (additional hard disk space)

- faster processor

- high speed serial port expansion card

- high speed video expansion card

- large monitor

- higher speed modem.

FINDING OUT ABOUT ACCESS

Choosing access facilities

Once you have your computer set up, you will need to choose an access account so that you can dial the Internet. If you are like most businesses you will be looking for a **dial up** account. This means you are not permanently connected to the Internet; you simply connect to the Internet using a regular telephone call, made by the computer – you 'dial up' to the Internet. This means that one of your biggest expenses for using the Internet will be telephone costs. For this reason alone you should use an Internet access account that enables local phone calls to be made. In the jargon of the Internet you are looking for an access provider who has a local 'point of presence' or POP.

Finding an access provider

Companies that provide you with an access account to use the Internet are known as **access providers** or 'service providers'. Sometimes you will see them referred to as 'ISPs' – Internet Service Providers. Whatever they are called, you need to find out about companies which have a local POP, which is not that difficult. *Yellow Pages* now has an 'Internet Services' category which should include local access providers, or point you to computer companies that can help in your area.

Alternatively, look in the main Internet magazines. These contain listings of access providers and indicate whether or not there is a local POP for you. In some countries, however such listings are not widely available. So, to find out your nearest access provider you should visit your local computer shop. Almost every computer dealer should know where the local access providers are.

Settling on an access provider

There are a number of things you need to consider, other than getting an access provider who has a local POP and can therefore keep your phone bills down. Before making your final decision take into account:

- size of the access provider

- modem to user ratio

- registration fees

- on-going fees

- software provision

- user support.

Size of provider
Anyone can become an access provider. All you need is a modern computer, a bit of common sense, a couple of modems and a special telephone line. All in, you can set up an access provider company for about US$25,000; not much to start up a potentially international business – and you can get your money back within a couple of months. So, it's not surprising that some enterprising people have set up Internet access companies in their spare bedroom. Good luck to them. But these small firms do have a problem, particularly as the Internet grows.

Small access providers – the home based ones and those which have been spawned from local computer firms – often cannot meet the demand. They do not have sufficient staff to provide high levels of customer support and their ability to have hundreds of people on line at any one time is limited. Such companies are excellent, however, for personal users – people who want to access the Internet after work for hobbies or for education. So these companies do have a valuable place in the Internet world. But for serious business use they are sometimes limited. So, go for a bigger firm, preferably one with a well known name.

Modem to user ratio
This is a reflection of the size of the company. The more customers an access provider has, the more lines and modems it needs. If it has a low ratio of modems to users, you may well have to wait to get connected to the Internet. For serious business use you need an access provider who lets you have **instant access**. That means a high ratio of modems to users. Most access providers publish their ratios as it is a means of helping you identify the best company to opt for.

Registration fees
Companies will usually ask you to pay a fee to register with them. This fee covers the initial administration of setting up your account *etc.* Some companies charge a large initial fee and then low ongoing fees. Others

charge larger ongoing fees, but no set up charges. Some companies charge a one-off cost for life. You have to make the choice according to your company's economic position. However, if you are going to be using the Internet more than a couple of times a week, go for the firms that have higher initial charges and lower ongoing costs. This makes your per minute usage costs lower.

Ongoing costs

Some companies will charge you fees on a monthly basis; others on an annual basis. Some charge you per minute, based on the length of your connection time. Generally, you get lower fees if you pay annually in advance. Those that charge you per minute can work out very expensive. You will almost certainly underestimate the amount of time your company will be connected to the Internet. If you budget for a particular amount of fees based on the 'per minute' charge, you could end up paying considerably more: often more than would have been the case with monthly or annual billing.

Software

The set up fees that you pay the access provider should include the costs of the relevant computer **software** that you need to whiz around the Internet. Nowadays, you should expect either a program called Netscape or one called Microsoft Internet Explorer. These programs work on all the mainstream business computers and are now really the only two programs around. There are others around, but if your access provider has either of the two main programs, you will have made a good choice.

One of the key things to ask a potential access provider is whether or not they **configure** the software for you. If they do, great. If not, you will have a fair amount of work to do for yourself and unless you are familiar with computers, this can be very offputting. It is often worth paying slightly higher set up charges to get your access provider to configure the software for you.

User support

Ask potential access providers what kind of support they provide. To new users the Internet can be a daunting prospect. Having a guiding hand can be very useful in the early days. Some companies only provide support during office hours, which may be fine for your business. But what if you want to access the Internet during cheap telephone periods, after office hours? If no support is available you may be scuppered.

Again, you pay higher ongoing fees for higher levels of support, so you need to balance your finances with your requirements.

Using international on-line services

There are a number of international on-line services that provide access to the Internet, often through a local POP. These on-line companies are commercial concerns that have their own databases you can access in addition to getting onto the Internet. Around the world there are three key on-line services providing Internet access. These are:

● AOL

● CompuServe

● Microsoft Network.

There are also nation specific on-line services, such as UK Online. All of these on-line services provide a host of features of their own, in addition to Internet access. They have electronic mail, databases on all sorts of topics and special interest groups for discussions and information exchange. However, even added together these on-line services do not provide anywhere near the amount of material that is available on the whole Internet. That is why they provide access to the Internet as well.

If an on-line service provides you with a specific business need, then it will obviously be of use. However, if you are only using the service as a means of getting onto the Internet, think carefully. Some on-line services can work out more expensive for Internet access than using a direct link through an access provider. This may not always be true – it depends upon the amount of time you will be using the Internet compared with the on-line company's own services. At the outset that can be difficult to judge.

One way of finding out is to use a **free trial membership**. These provide time limited access to the on-line service and the Internet. Such memberships appear on disks stuck to the covers of computer magazines. Every month at least one magazine carries such a disk. They are a useful way of finding out what each on-line service has to offer and also what is available on the Internet for your business.

CHOOSING YOUR TELEPHONE SERVICE

Having chosen your access provider and set your computer up for optimum Internet usage, you need to consider the kind of **telephone line** you will use. There are three main kinds:

1. Standard telephone line.

2. ISDN.

3. Leased line.

Standard lines

For the vast majority of businesses a standard telephone line is all you need. It is cheap, it works and it is widely available throughout the world. When talking to access providers they may refer to your line as POTS. This is jargon that stands for Plain Old Telephone Service, basically the ordinary, day to day, telephone system! For the best usage, make sure the line is dedicated to Internet use – don't go through a switchboard, for instance. Also, don't have fancy services such as 'Call waiting'. These can cause problems with your connection. Just have an ordinary telephone line linked to your computer dedicated to your Internet activities. You will also, therefore, easily be able to monitor usage of the Internet and analyse your costs. This could be important in companies where a number of staff are allowed to gain access to the Internet; you wouldn't want them spending your money on accessing the Internet for personal reasons.

ISDN

ISDN stands for Integrated Services Digital Network – jargon for a new kind of telephone line that is completely digital. Standard telephone lines include some old and some new technology. ISDN is all new technology – apart from the cable! ISDN has many advantages as well as some disadvantages. You will need to weigh these up carefully in your own case.

Advantages

● Each line is effectively a double line allowing you to use the Internet and make a phone call at the same time.

● Connections are very fast indeed, making call charges much cheaper as you may be connected for a shorter period of time.

● Connections are very 'clean' with little room for the kind of interference you may get on ordinary lines; your connections are therefore less likely to have problems.

Disadvantages

● Set up charges for ISDN lines are higher than ordinary lines.

● Rental fees for ISDN lines are higher than ordinary lines.

● Access providers usually charge higher fees to ISDN customers.

● Your office needs to be relatively close to a suitable ISDN exchange.

● You may need to upgrade your computer even further to be able to use ISDN lines.

Leased lines

A leased line is a telephone line that is permanently 'open'. In other words you are making a single telephone call that lasts permanently – or until your lease expires! The line has no number and no one can make another call, in or out. Instead, the leased line allows your computer to be permanently connected to the Internet. Such lines are expensive and are only of real value to firms that are doing a considerable amount of Internet work, or whose business is centred upon the Internet.

GETTING READY TO GO ON LINE

Once you have chosen the kind of telephone service and selected your access provider you will obviously be keen to get going and explore the world of the Internet. However, try to take things slowly at first, even though you will be excited and interested to see what's on offer. The reason is that mistakes in the early part of setting up your Internet activity can play havoc with your business at a later date.

When you have everything ready to get on-line you need to think about the following things:

1. Who within your business will have access to the Internet?

2. Which computers will be used as Internet machines?

3. How will Internet access be logged?

4. Will there be a 'convention' for electronic mail addresses within your business?

5. Who will be in charge of the company's Internet programme?

6. Who will monitor Internet activity?

In other words, you need a **written plan** to guide you through your Internet usage. Simply getting hooked up and getting on-line isn't enough. To do so can be costly as it could waste staff time and could increase all sorts of expenses for your business. So, the first step in getting on-line is writing your Internet plan.

Internet planning

Without some kind of plan for using the Internet your business could soon be on the rails. Either you or your staff will become hooked into the Internet and will waste precious time on non productive, but highly interesting, activities. You will also increase your telephone call costs considerably.

Your re-written business plan should give you a guide as to where to go with your Internet plan. You will certainly need to make someone within the business responsible for Internet activities. The Internet should not be seen just as another minor activity. It is likely to be a highly valuable business tool in your firm, so manage it properly. Someone who is in charge of your company's Internet activities will therefore be able to ensure that you meet the requirements of your re-written business plan.

The Internet manager will also be able to draw up plans for how and when the Internal will be accessed, who will do it *etc*. These plans will be vital to you being able to ensure that your company gets the best out of the Internet. Without such written plans your Internet usage could be doomed and your company could collapse.

A key decision for the Internet manager is how you will be addressed in **electronic mail messages**. If everyone in the company has a different style, the outside world might not realise that you are all working together. Consistency is important and you need to decide how you will be addressed right at the start. Once you start setting up your software ready to go on-line, you will be asked for the details of 'email' addresses. If you haven't got some kind of plan at the outset your address system could be a shambles.

Deciding on email addresses

An electronic mail address is quite easy to understand. At first sight it looks a bit daunting but it is actually quite straightforward. For instance, take my address:

---

gjones@zoo.co.uk

If you look at the address form right to left (backwards!) it all becomes obvious. The 'uk' clearly signifies I am based in the UK. If I were in the Netherlands, for instance, the last two letters would be 'nl'. The only country that doesn't have national letters is the USA. The Internet system assumes that if you don't have a country identifier you must be from the USA. Biased, I know, but there it is.

The next part of my address is 'co'. This is short for 'company' and essentially indicates that my address is a business one. The word 'zoo' is the name of that business – it identifies the location of the computer where my mailbox actually exists. (Zoo is a British based access provider.)

The @ sign means 'at' and it shows that the material to the right of the sign is the location of the mailbox, whereas the text to the left is the particular mailbox identification.

Clearly 'gjones' is a specific identification of my mailbox. But what if there was already another 'gjones' whose mailbox was at 'zoo'? We couldn't share the same name, so my mailbox might have been 'graham@zoo.co.uk' or some such alternative.

Being consistent

For individuals, conflicts for electronic mail addresses can easily be resolved. For companies it may not be so easy. That's why you need to develop a policy. It may be that you decide all your staff should have their mail addressed to their first name only, without surnames. Or it may be that you want surnames and departments listed as the text that appears before the @ sign in the address. Whatever you decide, consistency will help everyone else on the Internet send mail to the right people. It will also mean that your company and its staff are much more easily identifiable. So choose your electronic mail addresses with care – even before you dial up for the first time to the net.

SETTING UP THE SOFTWARE

Having decided on electronic mail addresses and the way your Internet activities will be managed you are ready to set up the software that came from your access provider. It cannot be emphasised enough that you should read the instructions a couple of times before setting up the software. Mistakes at this stage are often difficult to rectify, unless you are particularly expert at computers. So, read the instructions that came from your access provider and call their help line if you do not understand anything.

Tailoring the software to your needs

Following the instructions to the letter, install the software and set it up according to your needs. You will want to enter your electronic mail address, for instance. You should also alter any pre-set preferences so that they match your requirements. For instance, some programs may pre-set the interval for checking for electronic mail to every ten minutes. If you only receive one email every week, this continuous dialling up to the Internet can be expensive, not to say time wasting. Changing the interval to say every 720 minutes would mean that your computer would only automatically dial once a day, unless you had already done so.

Check such features carefully before using the Internet. However, one piece of real caution. Don't change anything you don't understand! This can lead to all sorts of trouble unless you really do understand computers.

Going live

Once you are ready, make sure your modem is switched on. It's a good idea to leave these on all the time; they don't use up much electricity and it's no more problematic than leaving your phone switched on. With your modem on and ready to go you can dial up to the Internet. Follow the instructions with your software and away you go.

You will almost certainly receive some welcoming electronic mail as well as being faced with the 'home' of the access provider that you are using. From there you can visit all sorts of destinations around the world. Some should have been pre-set for you by your access provider and you might like to explore these for a while.

FINISHING YOUR FIRST SESSION ON THE INTERNET

When you have had a chance to explore the software and the various facilities of the Internet, you should quite your program (often called a **browser**). Depending upon the type of computer and the type of browser software you have you might or might not still be connected to the Internet! One of the common first mistakes made by newcomers to the net is to continue their access telephone calls for longer than necessary. In many instances quitting the browser software does not disconnect you from the telephone. So check carefully: you may find there is no automatic disconnection.

If you are not automatically disconnected, somewhere you will find a 'disconnect' or 'close' command in the software your access provider gave you. If in desperation you switch off your modem you will be disconnected, but your computer may think you are still connected. That can lead to problems with your computer, so always use the proper commands.

CHECKLIST

1. You need a computer, a modem, a suitable telephone line and preferably a printer to let you physically connect to the Internet.

2. You also need an access account to get onto the Internet. Such accounts can be obtained in a wide variety of ways, so check carefully the options available. Payments in advance usually work out cheaper than paying as you go.

3. Prepare a written plan for the way your business will use the important tool of the Internet. *Adhoc,* ramshackle usage will do you no good in business terms and will also waste time and cost money. Ideally, your business should have an Internet manager to be responsible for the company's Internet activities.

4. Before going on-line for the first time, check all the documentation and prepare your mailbox addresses. Follow the access providers' instructions and remember to disconnect from the service properly once you have finished your call.

CASE STUDIES

Singapore finance firm changes tack

Mr Lee runs a financial advisory service from Singapore. He employs eight people and his business advises international investors on the 'tiger economies' of the Far East. His company has just started trading on the Internet, yet within a couple of months he has revised the way he does his Internet business. This is because he spent more time on administering his company's Internet activities than he imagined. For instance, his staff initially became hooked on the Internet and looked for all sorts of opportunities for business. That meant their existing, traditional business began to suffer.

Mr Lee had to spend a great deal of time ensuring his staff used the

Internet only for the proportion of time that it warranted. After just a month he decided to make one of his staff, Miss Ho, responsible for Internet activities; she manages the entire operation and ensures that staff only use the Internet where appropriate. Mr Lee has been freed up to get on with running the company and the remaining staff are able to get on with their work, without creating a backlog. Meanwhile, Miss Ho has enabled the company to exploit new avenues of business thanks to the Internet.

Australian graphics firm increases expenditure

Mike and Bob are two graphic artists who run their own business from Perth. The Internet was hit upon as the answer to their problems in communicating with clients on the other side of Australia. Until they decided to use the Internet, Mike and Bob had depended upon the Australian post to get their designs to clients in Melbourne and Sydney. That was comparatively expensive and time consuming. With the Internet, designs could be on customers' desks within minutes and the local rate phone calls would be cheaper than the postage rates.

However, a month after starting to use this system, Bob and Mike couldn't understand why their costs had actually increased. Although they only used the Internet a couple of times a day, their phone bills had increased significantly – far higher than their postage costs would have been prior to using the Internet. They employed a computer consultant to try and find out what was wrong. He discovered that Bob and Mike were sending their electronic mail messages correctly, but were only quitting out of their Internet mail program, not disconnecting from the Internet. For a two minute call, they had often been on-line for hours. They simply had not realised they needed to check that they were disconnected from the Internet.

Now they know this, they are much more careful and even got the consultant to come up with a method by which disconnection was automatic, saving them any future trouble.

DISCUSSION POINTS

1. Would you use an access provider or an on-line service for your company's Internet activity?

2. Who would you use in your company to be your Internet manager? Do you need to employ an additional member of staff?

3. In what way would you ensure your company has a consistent presence on the Internet? Would you write an Internet style guide for electronic mail?

3
Marketing your Business on the Internet

For most businesses, the Internet presents an excellent opportunity for marketing. You can let anyone in the world who has Internet access know of your existence. At the end of 1996 there were about 45 million companies and individuals hooked up to the Internet and the number grows by tens of thousands every day. Analysts predict that every business in the world will have Internet access in the next three or four years.

Advantages of marketing on the Internet
Using the Internet for marketing has a number of significant advantages:

- wide access to potential clients

- clients find you – you don't have to search for them

- costs are small compared with traditional marketing methods

- you can track your customers and easily identify real interest in your business

- you can make your marketing activities of practical help to potential customers, creating loyalty

- you can make your marketing activities much more interesting than traditional methods.

Disadvantages
Of course, there are some disadvantages to marketing on the Internet:

- not all your potential customers use the Internet

- you spread your message worldwide even if you don't want to

- you have to learn a new, computerised way of marketing

- the competition is much more easily located by your customers

- you have to use other methods of marketing as well as the Internet; most businesses cannot rely on the Internet alone.

Before you can benefit from Internet marketing, you need to decide how your current marketing activities will be helped by the Internet. Which of the advantages can you utilise and which of the disadvantages can you negate? Only by writing a marketing plan, or adapting your existing marketing plan, will you be able to exploit the facilities of the Internet properly.

WRITING A MARKETING PLAN

If you simply add the Internet to your existing marketing activities and say it is part of 'the mix' you provide, you will not exploit it effectively. The Internet needs to be properly integrated within your current marketing activities if you are to derive benefit from it. For some companies, the Internet will be only a minor part of marketing; for others it will be central and your company may even exist only because of the Internet. Most businesses will fall somewhere in between these two extremes. Hence the importance of a **marketing plan**.

There are plenty of good books on writing marketing plans and you can find a basic guide in my book, *How to Start a Business from Home*. In principle you need to write down the methods you are going to use to reach your customers and potential customers: advertising, direct mail, public relations, posters, Internet pages, leaflets, point of sale material and so on and so on. Consider all the potential methods of marketing your business, including the Internet, and note their advantages and disadvantages for your business.

Checking out the competition

Check out what the competition does. How do your competitors use the Internet, if at all? What services and products are your competitors offering and at what prices? How do your potential customers view your competitors? Find out as much as you can about your competitors before writing down your marketing plan. To exclude competitor information from your planning at this stage will mean your plan is likely to fail.

Checking out your customers

Also, find out as much as you can about your potential and actual customers. What do they want from you? How do they perceive you? And what proportion use the Internet? How many of those who use the Internet would deal with you directly over the Net rather than use traditional methods? Again, finding out this kind of information at the outset of your Internet activities is vital. It is no good setting up a wonderful Internet presence if your customers will not use it.

Reaching your customers

Now you need to find out some information on how you might reach your customers. Taking everything you have learned so far into account, do some research on costings. Find out how much it costs to advertise, to produce direct mail leaflets and so on. Also get some information on the costs of using the Internet. Most local Internet magazines include tables of costs from the leading Internet access providers in your area.

Having assembled all the essential information you can write your plan. You can decide which customers you are going to target with which products and services. You can decide how you are going to reach them and how you are going to sell to them. Write all of this down, read it, re-write it and eventually produce your definitive marketing plan.

Keeping flexible

Be warned though. Make your plan as flexible as possible. Many businesses fail because they produce rigid plans that cannot adapt to the changing world around them. They blindly follow their written plans – because it is their plan – and then wonder why they fail. The Internet is a very fast moving and rapidly changing marketing environment. It is absolutely essential that your Internet marketing plans are as fully flexible as possible. Nothing should be in tablets of stone. Perhaps a 'menu' of options is best so that you can pick and choose according to changing circumstances.

RESEARCHING YOUR MARKET ON THE INTERNET

One of the key parts of your business plan will be **market research**. The Internet itself is a valuable tool for performing market research. By using the Internet for this part of your plan you will be able to:

● assess the size of the market

- gain market statistics

- discover academic research on your market

- find out details about competitors

- obtain price data.

In fact, the Internet can be used to find out a considerable amount about your own market. So even if your company doesn't invest in an Internet presence, you can still gain from the Internet by using it as a market research tool.

Planning your research

Whenever you use the Internet, prepare some kind of written outline as to what you want to do. This may be a few scrawled notes on a yellow sticky notepad, or it may be a more in depth analytical document prepared on your word processor. Either way the principle of advance planning is important. Decide what you want to find out, the key words that relate to the topic and any company or product names you want information on. If you do not write all of this down in advance you will waste time when connected to the Internet. That will lead to frustration and, importantly, increases telephone call charges. In some cases, it will also lead to extra access charges if your provider bills you by the hour. Working out in advance what you want to find out from the Internet will save you time and money.

Searching the Web

Once you have decided what you want to research you can connect to the Internet. For most businesses, the best place to search is on part of the Net known as the **World Wide Web** or WWW or W3 or 'The Web'. This presents information in a graphical and textual format, much like an ordinary magazine page. However, you can use your computer mouse to click on key words, pictures, logos and so on to transport you to other pages, anywhere else around the Web. For instance, you can connect to a Web page that resides on a computer in one country, click on a key word and view a page from another document that is on another computer, somewhere else in the world.

As an example, imagine you are trying to find out about international travel facilities. The 'home page' of Air Canada allows you a number of options. One of these is to find out information about hotels. Within three

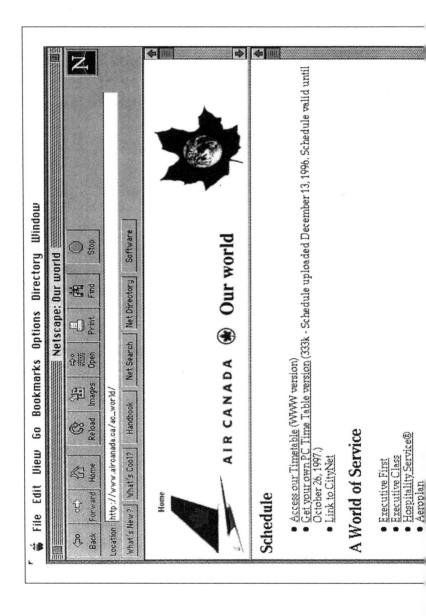

File Edit View Go Bookmarks Options Directory Window

Netscape: Our world

| Back | Forward | Home | Reload | Images | Open | Print | Find | Stop |

Location: http://www.aircanada.ca/ac-world/

| What's New? | What's Cool? | Handbook | Net Search | Net Directory | Software |

Home

AIR CANADA ✻ **Our world**

Schedule

- Access our Timetable (WWW version)
- Get your own PC Time Table version (333k - Schedule uploaded December 13, 1996. Schedule valid until October 26, 1997.)
- Link to CityNet

A World of Service

- Executive First
- Executive Class
- Hospitality Service®
- Aeroplan

38

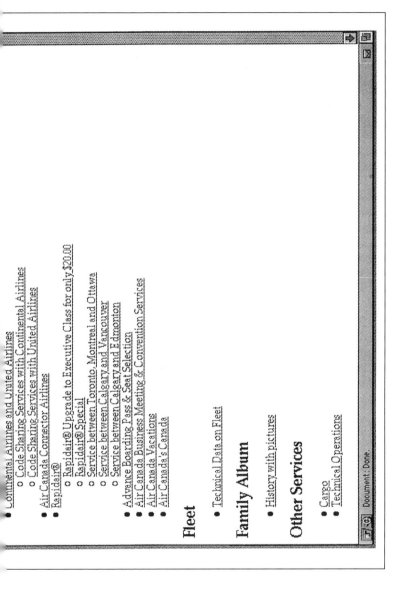

Fig. 2. Big business is already on the Internet: Air Canada's page can take you around the world.

mouse clicks and about 20 seconds, you can go from viewing the Air Canada page to reserving a room at the Conrad International Treasury Casino Hotel in Brisbane, Australia. This dynamic nature of the Web is one of its key attractions.

Knowing where to start

Even with your keywords written down, discovering links like the one between Air Canada and Hilton Hotels can be time consuming. And besides, how do you know where to begin the search? Thankfully, starting out on your market research activity is made easy by a number of systems known as **search engines**. These are highly sophisticated computer programs that allow you to search the entire World Wide Web for information that matches your interests.

The most popular search engines on the Internet are:

- Alta Vista

- Excite

- Infoseek

- Lycos

- NetSearch

- WebCrawler

- Yahoo!

Each of these search systems maintains a database of what is available on the Web. These databases are kept up to date by access providers, companies and individuals who publish their own material on the Web and by the search companies themselves. When you use the search system, the database is scanned to find pages that contain material that matches your interests. Because the databases are not identical, it is worthwhile using two or more search engines at any one time to be sure that you have retrieved as much information as possible.

Using the search engines

Have your list of key words and interest topics to hand. Select your search engine and enter the key words into the box. Be sure to use fairly well defined keywords and avoid common words. For instance, to search for information on paint manufacturers based in Australia, don't just enter the word 'paint'. You will get tons of data back that you don't need, including information on the paintings on the Colombus Doors of the US Capitol Building in Washington DC!

Instead, use search terms like 'paints and coatings Australia'. This will find just one entry, the Surface Coatings Association of Australia – just what you want – instead of over 520 entries on 'paint'. So, consider your search terms carefully. In this example you will see the word 'coatings' was added as 'paint' is too broad a term, including leisure painting as well as industrial manufacture. The industry refers to itself as being in the coatings business; using this term helped narrow down the search substantially and locate a key source of market information.

Checking search lists

Each of the search engines will provide you with a list of Web pages that match your key words as well as some brief details about what appears on those pages. Not all of the pages will be suited to your particular piece of market research. You will waste time and money if you try to look at every Web page that the search engine lists. So, your first step is to check the list. Indeed, for long lists it is wise to save the lists on your computer hard disk, disconnect yourself from the Internet and then read through the lists. This will minimise your phone costs. Once you have identified the most relevant pages to you, reconnect to the Internet and call up those pages only. Trawling through dozens or even hundreds of pages is fascinating, but hardly productive and runs up large phone bills.

FILING SEARCH INFORMATION

Having established exactly which pages you need to look at, reconnect to the Internet and retrieve those pages only. To do this, click on the names of the pages in the search document that you saved earlier in the process. You simply open this document using 'Open' from the 'File' menu. Saved Web pages include all of the necessary 'hot links' to enable you to jump from one part of the Net to another. You don't have to be connected for these hot links to exist; though you do need to connect for them to work, of course.

If the list of Web pages in your original search is quite long it may be quicker to simply type in the address of the page you want. You can then go directly to the page without having to scroll through your search list, thus saving time and money.

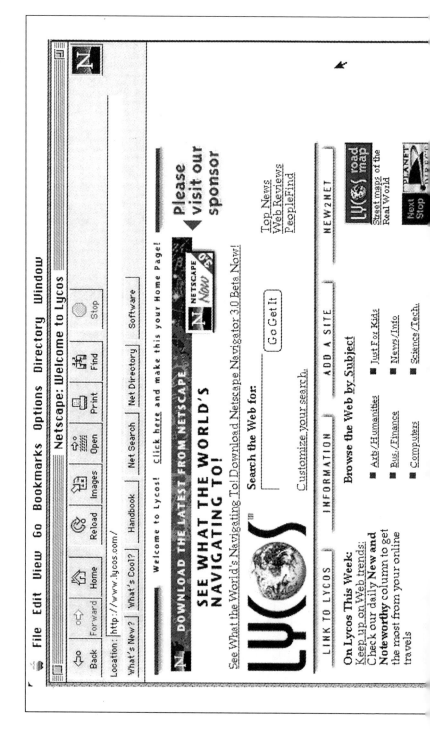

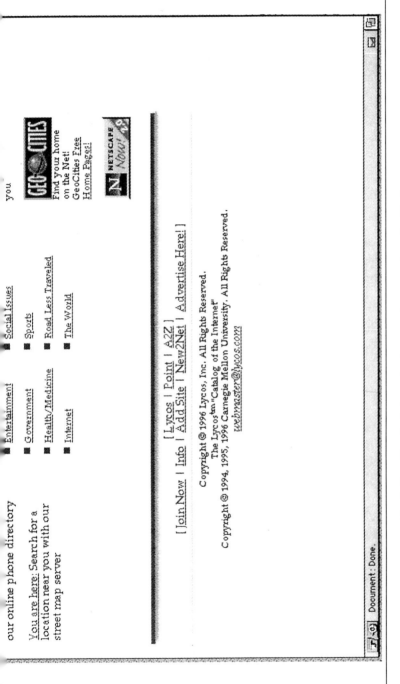

Fig. 3. Searching for information is easy using a search engine like Lycos.

43

File Edit View Go Bookmarks Options Directory Window

Netscape: WebCrawler Search Results for: home working

| Back | Forward | Home | Reload | Images | Open | Print | Find | Stop |

Location: http://www.webcrawler.com/cgi-bin/WebQuery

| What's New? | What's Cool? | Handbook | Net Search | Net Directory | Software |

Download

SHAREWARE.COM
NOW. Click here.

A SERVICE OF
c|net

WEBCRAWLER
Search before you surf!

Search Browse Special Add URL Help

home working

Search

Documents 1-100 of 516694 matching home working.
Show summaries for these documents.

IHA Charter Member Benefits
The Home Page of the Working Goldens
Ki-Net - New Organisational Structures for Engineering...
WIAC Johnstown 6 - Family First

44

| Category Listings |
| DAPTF-SW. U.S. Working Group Home Page |
| Chapters 1-4 of The Open Road |
| gopher://cwis.usc.edu/00/LibraryResearch/Research/by.subj... |
| S&R Marketplace |
| working @home! |
| A Business Researcher's Interests: Management Information... |
| College Internet Design Working Group - Trinity College.... |
| The Voices of Colombian Women |
| Philanthropy Related Links |
| ftp://ftp2.cc.ukans.edu/pub/hmatrix/medlist03.txt |
| A man in need of hope! |
| The resource for people who work at home. |
| Rita Louise Home Page |
| plans design cad drawings |
| United Doberman Club Home Page |
| Cuba Working Group Home Page |
| Rec.antiques.radio+phono FAQ |
| Product Update |
| economia |
| ftp://ftp.halcyon.com/pub/FWDP/International/untrtstd.txt |
| The Democratic Party Platform |
| The Democratic Party Platform |
| new information bulletin |
| White Pages |
| FAQ: Canada to U.S. Immigration for Businesses and.... |
| ftp://ftp.halcyon.com/pub/FWDP/International/untrtstd.txt |
| FINWeb Home Page |
| Resources for working on the Web |

Fig. 4. Search for 'home working' and you will get more than half a million matching documents!

Understanding Web addresses

Like electronic mailboxes, pages on the Web have a unique address. These are sometimes referred to as **URLs** which stands for 'Uniform Resource Locators' – jargon for 'address'! For instance the URL of my access provider is:

    http://www.zoo.co.uk

Once again, read the address from right to left. This indicates it is based in the UK, is a company called Zoo and is on the World Wide Web. The two slashes on the left separate the address from a piece of code telling the computer what kind of protocol to use for transferring the data. 'HTTP' stands for 'Hyper Text Transfer Protocol'. Hyper Text is the name given to the items in Web pages that provide the hot links from one page to another. By clicking on a piece of hyper text the computers are instructed what to do. It is a highly sophisticated method of 'turning over' a page, or closing one document and opening another. It is all invisible to the user, so you need not worry about it. All you need to be concerned about is that your addresses will usually need 'http://' at the beginning if you are to be able to navigate the Net.

The Web is case sensitive, so be sure to copy addresses exactly, including capitals and lower case letters in appropriate positions. If you do not, the Internet computers will not be able to locate the pages you want. The address is that specific.

Retrieving the pages you want

Whether you use hot links or type in the Web address yourself you will retrieve a plentiful supply of material to help in your market research. It is tempting a read through it as you get it. But this wastes time and costs money. By all means scan down the pages – they may have useful links to other sources of information – but don't be tempted to read them word for word. Print them out as they arrive or save them for reading later. This will save your phone costs and will make your search faster.

It is also worth noting that the popular programs that allow you to use the Internet – the browser applications – will allow you to retrieve more than one page at a time – even from different parts of the world. The method for doing this varies from computer to computer and between different browser programs, so check the documentation and help files carefully. Retrieving more than one page at a time can save considerable amounts of time and dramatically reduce your Internet costs.

USING THE INTERNET MATERIAL

Once you have retrieved a variety of pages you can use the information in a variety of ways. You can:

1.   Store the data and use it as reference.

2.   'Bookmark' the page for future use.

3.   Email the page publisher for more information.

Storing the data

You can simply save the pages you need for future reference and open them at any time in the future with your Web browser program. If you are using the information in your own materials, though, be careful. The Internet pages are the **copyright** of the publishers. The Internet is covered by the same laws that apply to printed publications – a couple of test cases have now established this as fact.

Bookmarking pages

Web browser programs allow you to store **bookmarks**. These are hot links direct to the pages you want to refer to frequently. With the relevant page open in your browser (you do not have to connect to the Internet) choose 'Add Bookmark' from the relevant menu – this varies among browsers. The URL of the page will then be stored so that you can connect to it again in the future. This is a very valuable way of keeping your market research up to date when pages are subject to frequent updates. For instance, financial news pages are updated hourly and you can get the latest news by simply selecting the relevant bookmark for your particular page of interest. That way you don't have to continue searching, or keep re-typing the, sometimes long and complex, URLs.

Another way of keeping your market research up to date is to use one of the many available Web **page editing** programs. These allow you to construct your own 'home page' which will appear when you start your browser. This home page does not have to be on the Internet, it can stay on your own computer unseen by the rest of the world. However, your home page can have logos or key words, whatever you want, that act as hot links to your favourite pages on the Internet. You set up your own home page so that you can point and click at an item to take you direct to the part of the Internet you want to explore. This can save considerable time, particularly if you are using the Internet for ongoing market research.

SETTING UP YOUR OWN INTERNET PRESENCE

Once you have completed your market research and written your marketing plan, you will be in a position to set up your own Internet presence. Many people use the Internet – particularly the World Wide Web – only to market their business; they do not sell through the Net. Later in this book, you will be able to find out how to use the Internet for selling, but first let's take a look at how you can use the Net for marketing. To do this you need to set up some kind of presence – you need a shop window basically. Therefore you need to use your marketing plan to help you settle on what your shop window will display. What will actually appear on your opening Internet Web page? Who will the Web page be aimed at? Will your page provide links to other pages? If so, which ones?

As you can see, setting up your Internet presence involves even more thinking and planning than was needed for your company's marketing plan. Failing to plan your Internet presence properly will mean your marketing plan is wasted and you will spend money with little or no result. The Internet is littered with poorly planned pages and poorly presented companies. Don't fall into the same trap. It would be just as damaging as producing a badly printed leaflet, or a brochure that is sent to the wrong audience. Think carefully at the outset and your marketing will pay off.

Selecting material for the Internet

Your first decisions are likely to be based on what you want to include in your Internet pages. You might want to include:

Yes/No

company mission statement _____

company history _____

company profile _____

products and services offered _____

staff profiles _____

customer lists _____

testimonials from customers _____

hot links to customers' web pages _____

hot links to suppliers' web pages _____

hot links to professional or trade associations _____

hot links to relevant subject areas   _____

hot links to your access provider   _____

hot links to your web page designer.   _____

As you can see, it is a long list and not exhaustive. There are plenty of other areas of interest specific to your industry and business that may be suitable for inclusion in your Internet presence. Choose what you want with care. People do not have time to sift through pages and pages of material, no matter how interesting you might think it is. Also, the more material you include in your pages, the more storage space it takes up at your access provider – and that costs you money. Access providers and Web space providers charge by the megabyte. The more material you have stored, the more it costs you.

Choosing your hot links

You will also have noticed that you need to consider the **hot links** your Web pages should have. The Internet is a dynamic entity: if you do not include links to other pages on the Internet your company will lose out as it will not be taking full advantage of the system. People who visit your page will not find it useful if it has no links. That means you are unlikely to be 'bookmarked'. In other words, a page without links is as good as a badly targeted leaflet – it is effectively thrown away. So consider carefully which links you want and make sure you get accurate URLs for the ones you want to highlight.

Designing your Internet Web pages

There is nothing to stop you designing your own pages and there are plenty of Web page authoring programs available. However, stop and consider for a moment. Would you design your own corporate brochure or would you get a design company or print firm to do this? Would you design your own advertising or get an agency to do this? For most companies, the design is left to the experts. For some unknown reason, though, many companies believe they can design their own Web pages. This leads to poorly laid out pages that often take ages to download across the international networks. Many people give up trying to view such pages because they take so long. If you want good Web pages use a specialist design agency to help produce them. Such agencies advertise in the Internet magazines, on the Internet itself and are known to your access provider. Indeed, some access providers also offer this service.

Doing it yourself

For small companies, using agencies may be too costly and the design has to be performed in-house. If this is the case, make sure you get some design training first. Courses on Internet Web page design are advertised in the Internet magazines. For newcomers to the Web, they are essential. Poor Web page design is probably the number one reason why many pages do not get the readership the companies expect. Don't skimp on design; get it right at the outset and you will be rewarded with high readership figures, and therefore a higher visibility and better marketing.

PRODUCING YOUR WEB PAGES

To produce a Web page you need all of the text and graphics you are going to include as well as all the URLs you want to have as hot links. Your Web page designer can then lay out the pages as you want them and test them using a browser program. You can then view them, alter them and test them thoroughly before you give the final go ahead for publication. Two key things need to be remembered at this stage:

1.   Check the hot links work.

2.   Check your pages are legal.

Checking your hot links

Test all the hot links thoroughly before publication. Nothing infuriates Web users more than incorrect URLs within a page or hot links that just go nowhere. Equally frustrating are hot links that take you to pages that are slow to download. Put your pages through rigorous testing on a couple of different computers, preferably using more than one access provider. In this way you will be able to test how well your pages work under different conditions. Your access provider should do this for you if they are providing you with the complete package of Web page design, Web space rental and so on.

Checking your pages are legal

The second point to remember is that your pages need to be **legal**. You can libel people, perform copyright infringements and a host of other illegal acts, if you are not careful. The Web pages are publications, just the same from a legal standpoint as a magazine. If you are unsure about your pages, get them checked over by a lawyer before you publish them. There are even lawyers on the Internet who will do this for you. All you have to do is email your pages to them for a thorough check.

Once your pages are checked, you can get them published. To do this you simply let your web space provider have the file. You can send the file by email, on floppy disk, or using 'FTP' – File Transfer Protocol. FTP, the most popular method, involves you sending the file direct to the provider's computer without going through email. Your Web space provider will give you details of what you need to do.

CHOOSING YOUR INTERNET ADDRESS

Once your page is ready and available at your Web space provider it can be accessed by anyone in the world. However, to do this the page will need a URL – a Web address.These addresses are agreed internationally, you cannot simply choose one and use it. You have to get permission. Even though no one owns the Internet as an entity, there are now international agreements in place which ensure that addresses are fair and acceptable. For instance, say your company was called 'General Machinery'. You might be tempted to use 'GM' as the key part of your address. But that would conflict with 'GM', the more internationally known 'General Motors'. Hence your application would fail. Some people have tried registering popular names for addresses in the hope that they would become a valuable property that could be sold on to the company concerned. Such dreamers have failed in their mission because the companies have opted for better addresses or invoked trade mark infringement cases.

Whatever you choose as the key part of your address, remember it will have other elements giving a clue as to your destination. The final part of your address will have the country, such as 'uk', 'au' and so on. The exception is the USA which has no international identification on the Internet; if there is no country at the end of the address, it is the USA.

The second part of the address, from the right, will identify your particular type of organisation. These suffixes include:

co	company
com	commercial organisation (mainly US)
org	non commercial organisation
edu	educational establishment (mainly US)
ac	academic establishment
mil	military establishment
gov	government or government department

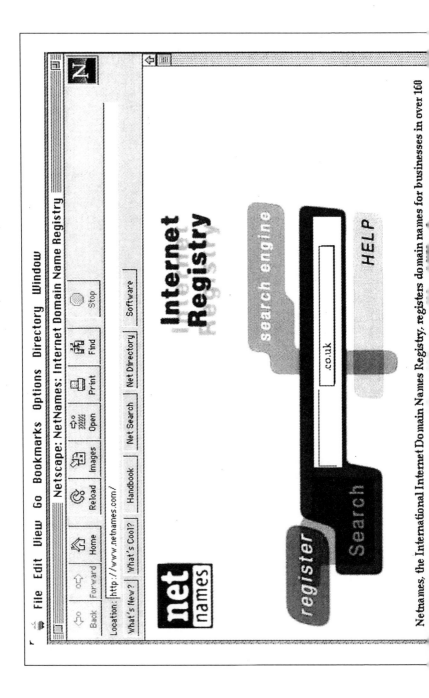

Netnames, the International Internet Domain Names Registry, registers domain names for businesses in over 160

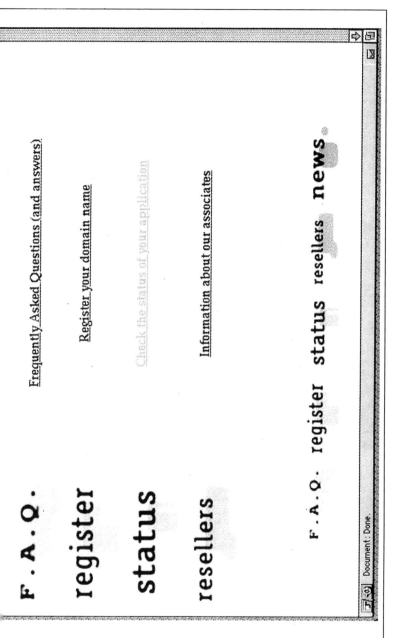

Fig. 5. You need to get an Internet name: one place to go is the net names registry.

Most business addresses include the 'co' abbreviation, indicating they are a commercial concern. The first part of the address for web pages will always be 'www'. So, the only part you can vary is the bit between 'www' and the 'co'. You will be required by the international naming committee to come up with a word that reflects your business. You will also need to come up with something that is easy to type and straightforward to remember.

Getting a URL

To obtain your chosen URL you need to **apply** for it. There are two ways of doing this. You can get your access provider to make an application on your behalf, or you can apply yourself. To make your own application you need to contact one of the naming agencies; these exist around the Internet and one of the most popular can be found at the following URL:

hhtp://www.netnames.co.uk

For many companies, though, it is easier to use their access provider to act on their behalf. You can get your access provider to rent you the necessary Web space and also register your URL. They set the whole thing up and make it as easy as they can for you. This is why choosing your access provider properly can pay dividends in the long run. A company that can take on all of your Internet behind-the-scenes work, allowing you to manage your pages and so the marketing, relieves you of a lot of headache-inducing hard work!

PUBLICISING YOUR PAGES

Once your pages are designed, allocated space at your access provider and allocated a URL, the world can start to view them. However, If people do not know about them, they can sit hidden from view forever. So, once your page is ready and available on the Net, be sure to publicise it. The people to let know include:

● search engines

● all the page owners you have hot links to

● all your customers

● all your suppliers.

Be certain to let every search engine know of your existence. Go to each search engine on the Internet and send them details of your URL. Each search engine home page has a button you can press to do this. By sending the search engines details of your page, anyone in the world making a search could then find your page, even if they didn't know your company existed.

Never forget to tell as many people as possible about your Web presence. Companies often forget to have stationery reprinted with details of email and Web page addresses. Don't let this happen. Publish your Web page address widely – on headed paper, business cards, leaflets, adverts, brochures and so on. Indeed, you will probably have already noticed that many companies now include their URLs at the foot of TV and press adverts. Take a tip from these big firms, publish your Web address as widely as possible. Otherwise you run the risk of having a Web page that is the world's best kept secret. If you have invested in developing good Web pages, let everyone know!

MONITORING WEB USAGE

Having your Web page published and available to read is one thing, but the Internet provides you with much more of a marketing tool. You can use the Internet to discover who is actually looking at your pages and for how long. You can even find out which pages interested which people the most. In this way you can build up a highly valuable mailing list of people who are clearly interested in your company, its products and services.

When you rent Web space be sure to ask for the **full reporting options** available. The provider will report back to you on who looked at your pages, when and for how long. You can then use this information to provide highly targeted material, thus attracting custom. The fact that the Internet can tell you who is looking at specific material is one of its key marketing attractions. If you send a leaflet out to a 1,000 homes, you know that by the law of averages 60 homeowners will read it – but which 60? With the Internet you don't have to send the material out, the potential customers come to you; but the difference now is that you know exactly who is interested and, more specifically, precisely what they are interested in.

Don't neglect the follow up activities involved in using the Internet. They could prove to be your most valuable marketing tool. You can build up mailing lists of potential customers whom you can target with special offers, for instance. Equally, you can use the information you gain to refine products and services to increase market share.

CHECKLIST

1. Before using any part of the Internet for marketing, be sure to integrate it properly into a written marketing plan.

2. Your marketing plan should be written only with the benefit of thorough market research. The Internet itself can be used for such research.

3. Get proper advice on setting up your own Internet presence. Particularly important is getting good design for your Internet Web pages.

4. Use an access provider or Web space provider to do the 'back room' work for your Internet activities, allowing you to use the Net to maximise your marketing initiatives.

5. Check that your Internet pages work and that they are legal before you publish them.

6. Monitor your Web pages properly. Use the detailed information from your access provider to increase market share.

CASE STUDIES

New Zealand despatch company has to start again

Andy runs a successful despatch company based in Wellington that wants to expand its operations. One of the key services Andy thinks he could provide is item tracking: his customers could call up his Internet page and discover within seconds where their package was, anywhere in the world. This would save them time. At the moment they have to call Andy, he then makes some checks and then has to call them back. Using a fully computerised system, linked to the Net, would allow Andy's customers to have instant access to information on their packages.

Together with a friend, Mike, who runs a computer firm, Andy develops his system and helps design his Web pages. He launches the new service amid a blaze of publicity and this helps to attract new customers. However, within a week Andy is working halfway through each night to try and rectify a whole host of problems. Mike, too, is working hard to help. The problem is that customers said the system was too slow. Andy was so keen on using pictures, rather than text, that Mike had helped him select a host of images from around the world. Rather than having a boring map of the world, thought Andy, his customers would get interesting pictures – the Eiffel Tower, the Grand Canyon and so on. True, the pages looked stunning, but they took ages to download. That was frustrating for the customers who tried to use the system. They spent less on phone calls when they called Andy and asked him to check things for them. The result was a wonderful but useless system. Andy and Mike have to completely re-think their pages and start again.

PR company boosts client list

Alison and Clive run a PR company in Ontario. They decide to use the Internet to market their services. Their company provides specialist PR facilities to people who run home-based businesses. They provide standard press relations, right through to complete event management. They set up their Internet pages so that each aspect of their work is separate: a page on press relations, another on company newsletters and so on. Each page is listed separately at each of the search engines and users can also hot link from one page to another using a visual menu strip across the bottom of each page.

Alison and Clive update the pages each month with new client lists and details of campaign successes. They hope that this will encourage users to bookmark the pages for reference. They also make sure they receive weekly reports on the usage of their pages. They use this information to build up a mailing list of potential customers on specific areas of their work. Every quarter these people are then sent an email 'newsletter' updating them on specific items of interest. In this way Alison and Clive can attract new, loyal customers to their company.

DISCUSSION POINTS

1. How would the Internet fit within your current marketing plans?

2. What other companies would you hot link to in your Web pages?

3. How could you use the monitoring information to improve your marketing?

4
Selling on the Internet

The Internet is a truly global marketplace and there is every chance you can sell your wares across the networks. There are very few services or products that cannot be sold over the Internet. Probably the only exception are intensely personal services, such as health consultations, where a hands on approach is needed. However, technology is already advancing so that healthcare professionals can examine patients over the Internet. Indeed, the technology already exists to allow robot performed operations to be controlled by surgeons who are thousands of miles away!

So, someone, somewhere in the world, is almost certainly using the Internet to sell the same kinds of products and services that your business produces.

FINDING OUT WHO BUYS FROM THE INTERNET

It may be a great idea to sell your products and services across the Net, but if no one uses the Internet to look for such items, you won't have any buyers. Equally, if your competitors take advantage of the Internet and you don't, you could find your sales fall in response to changes in the marketplace. So, you may well need to set up shop in the Internet, but how do you know if it will be worthwhile?

Knowing your target market
The market research described in Chapter 3 will help you get on the road to discovering potential customers. You may well have discovered that your competitors are already selling via the Internet. But there is more information that can help. If your products and services are aimed at the higher socio-economic groupings, people with disposable incomes, you are in luck. These are the most common Internet users. If your products and services are aimed mostly at women, you are out of luck. The vast majority of Internet users are men. Similarly, if you are aiming at either the elderly, or the very young, your chances of sales are limited because most of the Internet users are in their mid-30s.

According to one study conducted in 1996, almost six out of ten Internet users are aged 31 to 59 and they earned more than £25,000 per year. These users cite 'computing', 'science' and 'technology' as their main interests. The next level of interests are 'further education' and 'personal finance'.

So, the average Internet user is not a 'computer nerd', but a relatively well off male, middle to senior manager whose interests are intensely personal. That means anyone whose products and services fall outside this generalised Internet user is less likely to succeed in attracting sales. That does not mean you cannot sell your products since there are teenagers, old people and many women using the Net; it's just that there are fewer of them, thus limiting sales potential.

DECIDING WHAT TO SELL ON THE INTERNET

The products and services you sell on the Internet will depend on three key factors:

1. The potential market.

2. The products and services you have available.

3. The support you are able to provide internationally.

Offering support

Using the Internet you could sell your latest electronic gadget to someone in Tasmania, while you are in Quebec. But, if you can't provide maintenance or some kind of support scheme in Tasmania, you would soon get a poor reputation. You might say: 'sorry, there is nothing I can do from Quebec. Send it back through the international post and I'll see what I can do.' But before you had put the phone down, a message would be beaming across the Internet: 'don't buy from this Quebec company, they can't provide you with support'. So, if you want to maintain a good reputation and therefore promote your company, your products and services must be supported around the world if you are to sell them across the Internet. Indeed, this may well be a legal requirements in certain countries to which you sell.

For most services, international support is not a problem. You can provide telephone help lines, customer support pages on the Internet and so on. For businesses that are product orientated, servicing internationally may be more difficult, unless you are already a worldwide business.

However, do not neglect planning for customer service delivery. This element alone could determine your sales success on the Internet.

SETTING UP YOUR INTERNET SHOP

Once you have decided who your target customers will be and exactly what it is you want to sell to them, you can set out your stall. The information in the last chapter about marketing will be helpful when deciding how to set up your Internet site.

Looking at good design

Like any Internet page, your shop needs to be attractive, well designed and easy for people to use. Fancy graphics may look good, but they will deter potential customers as they can takes ages to download from your computer to one on the other side of the planet. Like well laid out retail stores, your shop needs to be easy to use – a good place for customers to spend their time, browsing through the items you have for sale. Don't make your sales pages look so busy they resemble an 'open all hours' 'we sell anything' kind of ramshackle store. The advice of a Web page designer will be worth the outlay if your shop is to attract and retain customers.

Make sure, though, your Internet shop pages have the following key items, clearly displayed;

● categories of products/services for sale

● illustrations of products

● prices

● means of payment

● hot links to full descriptions of products.

Making it easy for the customer

Essentially, your opening shop front page should give a clear indication of the exact categories of products and services you sell. Each of the individual items can have their own detailed page of description which can be jumped to from a hot link on the shop front. If you look at rival Internet shops, you will see that the opening pages are usually nothing more than a series of links to other, more detailed pages. In this way, customers can go direct to the items they want to buy without being distracted.

The downside, of course, is that, unlike a real shop, they won't be tempted to other offerings as they look around. You can overcome this with a variety of other hot links that lead from the page selected by the customer to other pages that may be of interest. In this way you can whet your customers appetite and attract them to anything else you are selling. Do not neglect the dynamic aspect of the Internet in your own shop pages. You will lose additional sales if you do.

Getting customers to buy

There are plenty of books available on attracting customers and how to sell. *How to Sell a Service* by Malcolm McDonald and John Leppard (Heinemann) is a particularly good book on the subject. Anyone opening up an Internet shop should follow the time-honoured advice on selling. Selling on the Internet is not vastly different from any other kind of sales activity, whether it is at a local bazaar or in a huge multiple retail store.

There are no 'tricks' to selling on the Internet and anyone who tells you otherwise is misleading you. From a sales perspective, the Internet is just another outlet, albeit a rather sophisticated one, with hard headed, practical, intelligent customers. So your sales techniques should be little different from the approach you would use for your customers generally.

What you do need to take account of are the special desires of Internet customers and the peculiar methods of Internet sales.

SIZING UP THE INTERNET CUSTOMER

As we have already established, Internet users are generally well-educated, intelligent and also have higher disposable incomes – there will be a greater proportion of gold card customers around than in the world at large. In other words, Internet customers are those which are most demanding: they expect more, demand higher levels of service and probably also complain more than the general population. Your Internet sales operation must be able to deal with such customers if your business is to survive.

UNDERSTANDING THE INTERNET SALES METHOD

The sophisticated customers who use your Internet shop will be making a special kind of purchase. They will not have seen or touched the product. They will not have been able to test it. If you are selling a service, they will almost certainly never have spoken to you and will not have 'sized you up'. In other words, Internet purchases are almost 'blind' and a considerable amount of trust is placed in you as a seller. This is an important factor to realise; your customers will expect higher levels of truthfulness and service than with most other methods of selling, where they have been able to test products or examine your claims more carefully.

Also, the demanding Internet customer wants their product or service 'now'. These people are used to getting information immediately and expect a similar high speed service for goods they buy.

Offering instant payment

The second important factor about selling methods on the Internet is that cash is almost non existent. Credit and debit card transactions can take place but because your customer may be thousands of miles away, in another time zone, using a different currency, you can't rely on cash. Cheque transactions slow down the proceedings, limit your cash flow and inhibit purchasers. Essentially, your Internet sales operation must allow people to make some kind of instant payment if you are to attract the maximum number of customers.

CHOOSING A PAYMENT SYSTEM

There are four main ways of accepting payment:

1. Credit and debit cards over the Internet.

2. Credit and debit cards by fax.

3. Cheques or credit/debit card details by post.

4. Vouchers.

Accepting credit cards over the Internet

The simplest and most straightforward way of collecting money over the Internet is with a **credit card transaction**. Many people are put off doing this because of the potential of 'hacking': the ability of anyone, anywhere in the world to locate your credit card details and use them fraudulently. This is a theoretical risk, rather than a practical one. In fact, sending your credit card details in the post or on a fax is considerably more risky. For a start, anyone from the most junior post room assistant to the boss can see credit card details posted or faxed into a firm. Yet, to track down your customers' credit card details on the Internet would need a highly intelligent, exceedingly determined and well practised computer whizz kid. Even so, there is sufficient hype about the so-called insecurity of sending your credit card details over the Internet that many of your customers could be put off if this is all you offer as a means of payment.

Using 'secure' methods
You can increase the level of security by using the **secure forms** method of payment. This is available in the most recent 'browser' applications and it considerably reduces the potential risk of a hacker retrieving confidential information. By using the 'secure' method of accepting payment you can increase your customers' levels of confidence. However, you can also limit the number of customers by doing this; not every browser has the ability to cope with this level of sophistication.

Accepting credit cards by fax
For the many people who are still reluctant to send their credit card details over the Internet you will need to provide an alternative method of payment. You can – even though it is less safe for your customers – accept payment via fax. The customer orders the products or services they require over the Internet and then faxes you their credit card details.

Accepting payment by post
This method is still used by some people even though it makes a mockery of the Internet. However, if you do not provide every avenue possible for payment you can limit your market. Some people seem happy to order goods and services over the Internet and receive confirmation of their order by email, yet won't pay using their computer. These people prefer to pay through the slower postal system, thus delaying their purchase.

Accepting voucher payments
Vouchers are a new form of currency that exists only on the Internet. Your customers can receive a supply of electronic vouchers that they spend on your products and services alone. Customers can swop vouchers amongst themselves, across the Internet, providing them with the same flexibility as cash. To buy vouchers customers can let you have their credit card details or send you a cheque – or even pay you in vouchers

that you can use elsewhere on the Net. By inventing your own vouchers you can dramatically increase the possibility of sales.

Such vouchers are not dissimilar to gift vouchers that you can buy in a range of retail outlets now. The main difference is that they are electronic and are transferable. Indeed, the rapid rise in the popularity of such vouchers has led Internet pundits to predict that they will become the most common form of payment.

HANDLING INTERNET ORDERS

When customers check out your Internet shop they must be provided with a simple and efficient way of ordering. Most Internet businesses use a straightforward order form. Products can be automatically added to the order form using hot links – as a customer selects a product by clicking on its name or picture, its details are added to the order. If you have a simple method like this, you will increase your sales. If you opt for a complicated method, whereby customers have to type in the details of the products themselves, you will lose orders. That's because it is time consuming and adds to customers' phone bills.

Your order form should include easy to use payment options and you should always ask for the customers' email address. In this way you can be sure to keep them up to date on the progress of the order. You can also build up a valuable database of people interested in your company's products and services.

Monitoring sales

Make sure you have a **daily plan** for dealing with orders. Make someone responsible at a specific time each day for checking what orders have come in and then processing them. Indeed, you will need to check the system regularly throughout the day. If you operate a large sales system, you may need to check the orders throughout the night as well – remember that is someone else's daytime on the Internet. The international operation of the Internet may mean you need to consider 24 hour sales systems. In any event, do not neglect your Internet sales operation: your customers will expect a swift response to their order.

BOOSTING SALES

Like all other sales operations don't forget things like:

● special offers

- sales promotions

- free gifts.

You can announce such special deals on your sales and marketing pages, via email or through other areas of the Internet.

Using newsgroups

One possibility is to make announcements of special offers *etc* in the 'news' area of the Internet. This is an enormous section of the Net and getting bigger every day. In fact, the amount of material added each day is roughly equivalent to 400 copies of the entire works of Shakespeare! Considering that each message on the newsheet is only a few lines, you can see how many people are using it.

Each section of the newsnet represents a specialist area. Hence you can find news groups for anything from complicated biochemical science to people interested in volleyball. You could post a message to the newsgroups which represent people interested in your products or services. Your message appears once and can be read by anyone who logs on to that particular newsgroup.

Using email

You shouldn't neglect the electronic mail method of boosting sales. You can let all your existing customers know about your special offers. Using the reports from your access provider you can also mail potential customers, people who have visited your sales pages but haven't yet bought. More details on using electronic mail for business can be found in the next chapter.

CHECKLIST

1. Analyse your potential customers' requirements before deciding what to sell.

2. Design your 'shop front' – your sales pages – with care. Make sure people can find their way around easily and quickly.

3. Entice people to look at other products and services you sell, using hot links from one page to the next.

4. Make it easy for people to order items using hot links and well designed forms.

5.   Make it easy for people to pay; consider Internet voucher systems for payments.

6.   Have an efficient, possibly 24 hour, sales operation to meet international demand.

7.   Don't neglect methods of boosting sales on the Internet.

CASE STUDIES

Hong Kong printing company offers easy international system

Kim runs a small printing company in Hong Kong and is keen to extend his services worldwide. He knows that print prices in Asia often beat prices in Europe and America. He is a general commercial printer and produces stationery, brochures and so on. Using the Internet he has been able to increase his sales by offering instant quotations, low prices and rapid turnaround. His sales page allows the customer to enter the details of their required printing – the number of pages, the colours, quality of paper and so on. Within seconds, the price is calculated by Kim's computer and sent directly to the person making the enquiry. If they like the price they can confirm their order, even sending computer-based artwork, directly over the Internet for reproduction by Kim's team and printing as necessary. Kim likes his system because it has made it so much easier for customers to get quotations. Also it has boosted his cash flow as a higher percentage of his orders are accompanied by credit card payment.

Scottish hotel loses out on Internet sales

A small family run hotel in the Scottish highlands decided to sell room space over the Internet. Users could dial in to the hotel's pages, look at pictures of the rooms and make a booking. However, the owners of the hotel, Mr and Mrs McMay, have seen the initial interest drop. They now know the reason and are changing their Internet pages to help improve the situation.

The main problem was that, because the Internet system was not linked in any way to the bookings system they couldn't confirm bookings immediately. Each day Mr McMay would check the Internet bookings, compare them with the reservations and then send email messages back to the potential customers saying whether or not they had been successful. He would then ask for a deposit by cheque. The Internet system was slower than booking by phone and lost him custom. Now, the system is linked to reservations, providing customers with instant booking ability plus discounts for advance payment by credit card. The improvements are beginning to pay off, but the initial Internet sales system was a waste of time and money.

DISCUSSION POINTS

1. What would be the best products or services for your company to sell over the Internet?

2. How would you best be able to collect payments?

3. What arrangements could you make to increase the level of service provided to potential customers?

5
Improving Business Communications with the Internet

The Internet was invented for communications. It was originally developed in the United States military and security services as a means of protecting information during the Cold War. In the event of a nuclear attack on the USA, important information could be speedily sent around the country from one site to another, thus enabling the USA to defend itself.

Later, the Internet was established amongst the academic world, first in the USA and later in other countries. The academic networks enabled researchers in universities and colleges to swop information and important details of their research quickly.

Only in the late 1990s has the Internet taken on its new role for business providing an outlet for marketing and sales activities. Because of the hype surrounding the Internet it is easy to forget that its roots lie in communication. The Internet offers the fastest and cheapest way to send information to almost anyone in the world. The recipient doesn't even have to be an Internet user. There are message services on the Internet that will take, say, your letter to someone in Australia from the Net, then relay it by local mail to the person you are writing to. In this way the mail is delivered faster and at lower cost.

So, even though many people extol the benefits of electronic mail, the Internet can provide you with a means of communicating with almost anyone, even if they do not have electronic mail themselves. For this reason alone, the Internet is well worth investigating as a central means of business communications.

You can use the Internet to communicate in the following ways:

- electronic mail
- telephone
- video phone
- faxes
- 'snail mail' letters.

USING ELECTRONIC MAIL ON THE INTERNET

Your access provider will have already asked you about your preferred name for your **mailbox** – the identifying tag that allows mail to be delivered accurately to you from anywhere in the world. Chapter 2 gives details of what you need to think about when choosing your electronic mailbox name.

Once you have an identifying name – an 'email address' – you can send and receive messages throughout the world. All you do is type your message on your own computer and press a button marked 'send'. It is as simple as that! Your message will first be saved on your own computer disk, so you can refer to it again – it's your file copy. A second copy is then sent across the telephone line to your access provider's computer. This recognises it as mail and sends it to the appropriate country, such as the USA if the last part of the mail address is 'com', or Australia if the last part of the mail address is 'au'.

Once a message has reached the relevant part of the world, the computers that make up the electronic mail backbone of the Internet set to work to locate the computers that represent the specific parts of the email address. Eventually, the message is stored on the computers of the access provider of the person you sent the message to. All of this searching and sorting can take seconds. It is not unknown for you to send a message to the other side of the world and receive a confirmation of its receipt within ten seconds. It really can be that quick.

Sending email messages

Your web browser program will have a method of sending electronic mail messages. This part of your program will let you send and receive email, including the ability to send computer files across the networks. For most people, the email facilities in web browser applications are sufficient. Only if you send a lot of mail or have sophisticated needs will you need a specialist mail program. There are plenty available and you can even buy them from sites around the Internet itself. For small businesses it is probably easiest to stick with the browser email facilities. Larger businesses will do well to use a specific email program as this allows improved internal communications, such as forwarding messages to other members of the staff and so on.

Building up an address book

Whether you use your browser program or a separate email program, be sure to build up your address book. This is a file that contains all the email addresses you use on a regular basis – it's a bit like your telephone

Netscape: Info You Requested

| Get Mail | Delete | To: Mail | | Re: Mail | Re: All | Forward | Next | Previous | Print | Stop |

Folder	Unread	Total
Inbox	0	204
Outbox	0	0
Sent	0	0

Subject		Sender	Date
Welcome!		Mozilla.	14/12/95 5:47 a.m
CONFIRMATION OF ...		Kimberly. Zilinski...	2/7/96 6:00 pm
Info You Requested		profitnews@info...	11/7/96 8:36 a.m
Re: Web space/dom...		nina.	11/7/96 1:09 pm
Re: Domain name		nina.	16/7/96 4:50 pm
Thanks for your regist...		Kagi Support TM	22/7/96 9:17 a.m
Command confirmati...		L-Soft list server ...	22/7/96 3:30 pm
You are now subscrib...		L-Soft list server ...	22/7/96 5:59 pm
▷ Output of your job "gj...			
Output of your job " ...		L-Soft list server ...	22/7/96 6:00 pm
Output of your job " ...		L-Soft list server ...	24/7/96 3:07 pm
AT&T HealthSite Regi...		siteadm@hdpw...	22/7/96 6:42 pm
▷ TAN, WAY TAN: Phot...		Adam Albright	22/7/96 6:42 pm
Re: TAN, WAY TA...		Geoffrey	23/7/96 3:56 a.m
Re: TAN, WAY TA...		Josh Sklar	23/7/96 3:59 a.m

Subject Info You Requested
Date: Thu, 11 Jul 1996 03:36:47 -0400
From: profitnews@infoback.com
To: Graham Jones <gjones@zoo.co.uk>

WELCOME! You are now subscribed to ProfitNews! If you ever wish to
unsubscribe, send e-mail with "Unsubscribe ProfitNews" in the subject

70

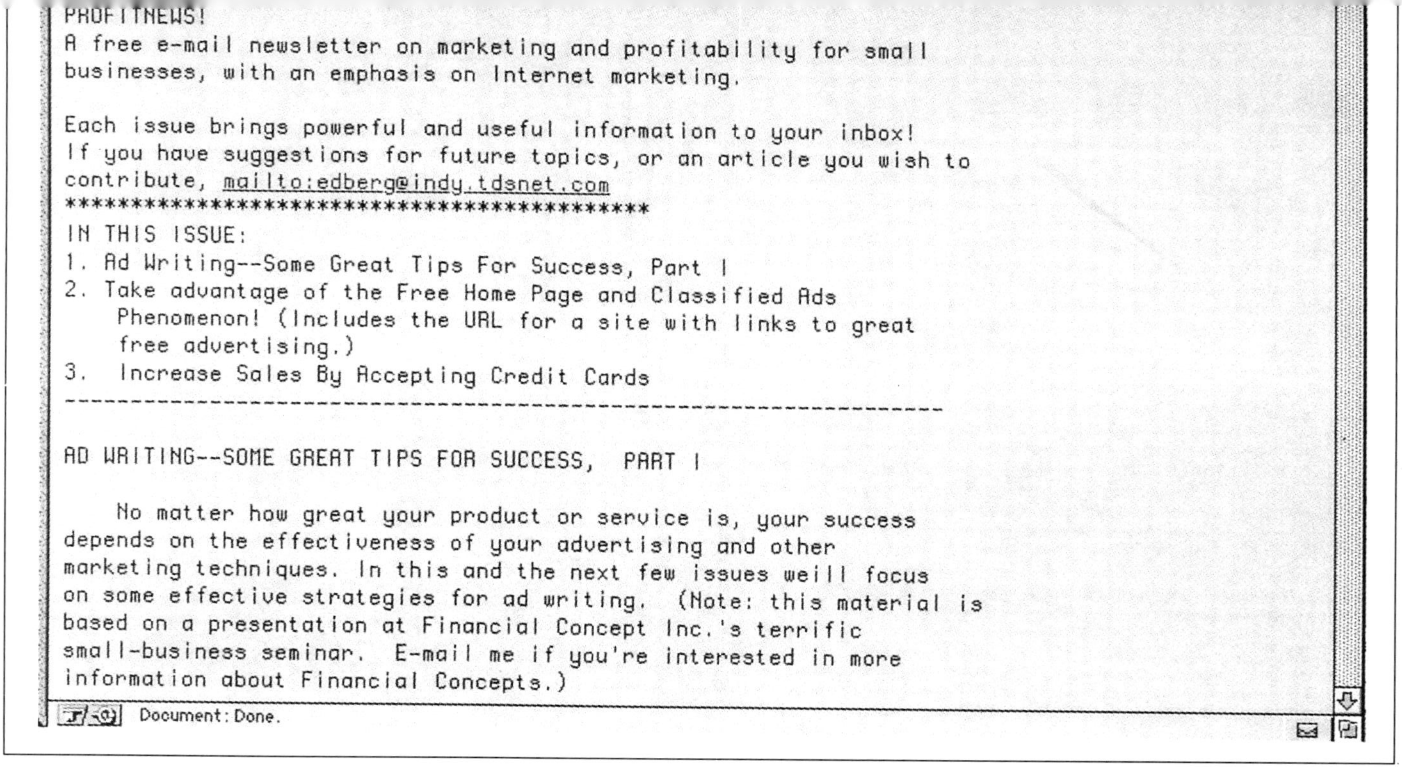

PROFITNEWS!
A free e-mail newsletter on marketing and profitability for small
businesses, with an emphasis on Internet marketing.

Each issue brings powerful and useful information to your inbox!
If you have suggestions for future topics, or an article you wish to
contribute, mailto:edberg@indy.tdsnet.com
****
IN THIS ISSUE:
1. Ad Writing--Some Great Tips For Success, Part I
2. Take advantage of the Free Home Page and Classified Ads
   Phenomenon! (Includes the URL for a site with links to great
   free advertising.)
3. Increase Sales By Accepting Credit Cards

AD WRITING--SOME GREAT TIPS FOR SUCCESS,   PART I

    No matter how great your product or service is, your success
depends on the effectiveness of your advertising and other
marketing techniques. In this and the next few issues we'll focus
on some effective strategies for ad writing. (Note: this material is
based on a presentation at Financial Concept Inc.'s terrific
small-business seminar. E-mail me if you're interested in more
information about Financial Concepts.)

Document: Done.

Fig. 6. A typical email session.

71

list of important numbers. Electronic mail addresses can be complicated and one minor typing error could lead to your mail not reaching its destination. So, save all the email addresses in the address book option of your program and this will avoid problems later. Also, be sure to back up your address book on a regular basis. You will have considerable problems trying to put together an email address book from scratch, should your original file be lost or damaged.

Saving telephone costs
Whenever you send email messages try, if you can, to prepare them all **off line**. In other words, prepare your messages, save them and then connect to the Internet to send them. Otherwise you could pay large telephone bills. Unless you only have to send one short message, your telephone call time will mount as the system waits for you to do the typing!

Similarly, when retrieving the email messages you are sent, it is tempting to read them as you get them. However, this increases your call charges. So, retrieve the messages, disconnect from the Internet and then read the email you have received. If you need to reply straight away to a message, you can compose your note, then reconnect to the Internet and send it. This is a much more efficient way of using the Internet and dramatically reduces call charges, particularly if your business has a number of Internet users in the office and uses email a great deal.

Developing an email policy
If your company uses email a great deal, you should develop a strategy and ensure that it is instituted company-wide. Otherwise you can waste time and money. Your strategy should include:

reasons for using email in
preference to 'snail mail' _____

reasons for using 'snail mail'
in preference to email _____

time of day when email
can be sent_____

time of day for checking
on received email. _____

In this way your company will reduce on-line call charges and will be more efficient. The Internet is a very tempting world. No sooner has an employee connected to send an email than they are searching for information on their favourite hobby. Before you know it, call charges are up and office efficiency and productivity are down. Having a well established and written email policy will improve things no end.

It's also worthwhile remembering that you need a policy even if you are self employed, working alone. You won't know if there are any messages for you unless you look. The email messages do not arrive by miracle on your computer with some kind of warning 'mail has arrived'. (That *is* possible using a combination of the Internet, pager systems and mobile phone technology, but let's not be too ambitious at this stage!) So the mail is 'invisible': you have to go and look for it. The speed advantages of electronic mail can be wiped out if you do not have a policy of checking your mailbox on at least a once-a-day basis. Otherwise, the people sending you messages could have used the ordinary postal system.

Finding out email addresses

It's all very well having the ability to send email, but who do you send it to? Conversely, if no one knows your address, how can they send you email? As you will have already guessed, the solution to this conundrum lies within the Internet itself. There are several systems that enable you to let the rest of the world know what your address is and through which you can find out other addresses.

Your Web browser should allow you to search for 'people'. Each browser approaches this in a different way. If you do not have a button marked 'people' or you are unsure, use your browser to open the following URL:

```
http://home.netscape.com/home/internet-white-pages.html
```

This page has hot links to a variety of search engines for email addresses. You can look up the addresses of individuals and categories of users as well. You can also register your own email address and provide some additional details. The search engines allow you to register your email address free of charge, though some directories charge you if you want more than a basic entry.

Finally on the topic of publicising your email address, don't forget to include it on all your stationery and all other promotional items. Many companies now include email addresses on their advertising; this is a good example to follow. The more people who have your email address, the better your use of the system.

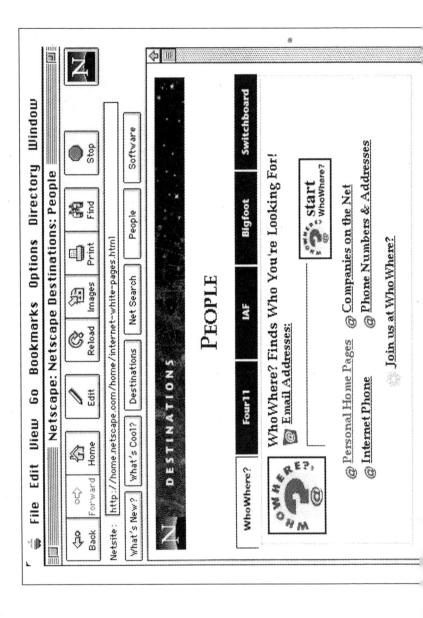

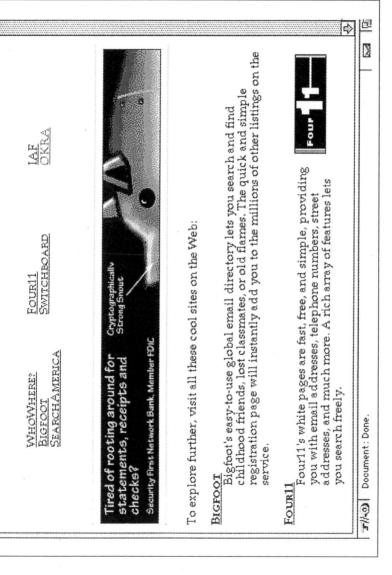

WHOWHERE?   FOUR11   IAF
BIGFOOT   SWITCHBOARD OKRA
SEARCH AMERICA

Tired of rooting around for statements, receipts and checks?

Security First Network Bank. Member FDIC

Cryptographically Strong Snout

To explore further, visit all these cool sites on the Web:

BIGFOOT

Bigfoot's easy-to-use global email directory lets you search and find childhood friends, lost classmates, or old flames. The quick and simple registration page will instantly add you to the millions of other listings on the service.

FOUR11

Four11's white pages are fast, free, and simple, providing you with email addresses, telephone numbers, street addresses, and much more. A rich array of features lets you search freely.

FOUR11

Document: Done.

Fig. 7. Finding people on the Internet is easy.

75

USING THE INTERNET FOR TELEPHONE CALLS

Because the Internet is linked through the various telephone networks of the world, there is no technological reason why you cannot use the Internet for making telephone calls. The reason why you may want to do this becomes obvious when you consider how you link to the Internet. If you have followed the advice earlier in this book, you will have chosen a local access provider. This means that **ALL** of your Internet activity is charged at local telephone call rates. If you use the Internet as a replacement telephone system you can call anywhere in the world at local call rates. If you make a lot of long distance or international calls, this can save you substantial sums of money.

Although this all sounds fine in theory, the practice is a little different. To use the Internet for telephone calls, the people you are trying to call must also be linked through the Internet. You cannot make calls to people outside the Internet world – yet! You also need special software, and in some instances adaptations to your computer, if you want to make Internet telephone calls.

For larger firms, Internet telephone calls make sense. They will save considerable sums of money on long distance and international calls. You can make a telephone call and send electronic mail to the person you are talking to at the same time. In this way you can swop information, discuss updates on data files all in 'real time'. You do not have to suffer any postal delays. However, you do have to be able to cope with making and receiving calls at odd times – the international nature of the Internet means business no longer happens in a strict 9 to 5 routine.

USING THE INTERNET FOR VIDEO CONFERENCES

Many firms arrange international video conferences. These allow 'meetings' to take place without the need for travel. People in different locations around the world can see and hear each other and engage in discussions, view presentations and so on. Such video conferences usually employ satellite telephone technology, which can be very expensive. The conferences are usually strictly timed to avoid excess call charges and to allow enough satellite time for other firms.

Using the Internet, companies can engage in video conferences at local call charges. Everyone involved connects to the Internet through their local access provider, hence international video conferences can take place extremely cheaply.

Keeping up-to-date with the technology

Be warned, though. The technology that allows this facility is at an early stage of development in the late 1990s. Pictures are slow and jerky and some access providers simply do not have enough 'space' on their system to be able to cope with the large volumes of data produced by video. Nevertheless, video conferencing over the Internet will become commonplace. You only need a cheap video camera and some software; indeed you can buy the complete kit from local computer retailers for less than £150.

So Internet video conferencing for business is real; it is here and now. However, for many businesses the technology is not yet advanced enough and it is therefore wise to keep an eye on this development rather than plan to use it for serious business. To keep up to date on Internet video conferencing, use your Web browser to open the following URLs:

http://www.videoconference. com
http://www.videoconf.com
http://www.wpine.com/cu-seeme.html

SENDING FAXES USING THE INTERNET

In the same way that you can make telephone calls on the Internet, you can also send faxes. This saves you money because every fax you send, anywhere in the world, is sent at local call rates – if you use a local access provider. Also, the recipient of your fax does not have to be an Internet user – you can send faxes over the Internet to anyone who has a fax machine. This facility alone is probably worth the annual cost of your subscription as it will save you vast sums of money if you send faxes long distance.

There are some extra charges to pay, depending on which kind of Internet fax service you use. You will either need to buy special software, or pay an Internet-based company to forward your fax on your behalf.

Whichever way you send a fax over the Internet it is always cheaper than sending faxes long distance and internationally using ordinary telephone lines. Pundits estimate that small businesses will save up to 30 per cent of their call charges and larger business can save around 50 per

Back Forward Home | Edit Reload Images Print Find | Stop

Netsite: http://www.outpost.net/

What's New? | What's Cool? | Destinations | Net Search | People | Software

Welcome to the OutPost Network, The Internet Post Office

Mail real greeting cards and letters — stamped
and delivered through the U.S. Mail
without ever having to leave your computer.

OutPost Network

- ♂ CARD SHOP
- $ BUSINESS
- ☼ SPOTLIGHT
- ◄ SERVICES
- ◐ ISSUES
- ☺ FUN
- ? HELP

Real Mail For Real People

New RubberChicken — Enjoy

Featured — CARD SHOP

Visit These OutPost Network Affiliates

the Love at First site

Garden Gate

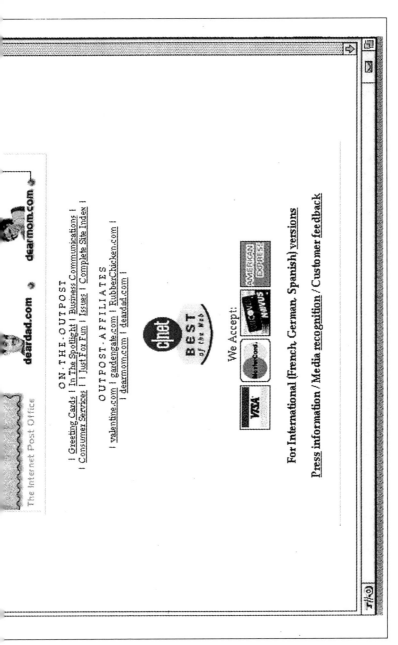

Fig. 8. If you don't like email you can still send ordinary post using the Internet.

cent. Faxing over the Internet is well worth investigating. To do so, use your browser application to go the following URLs.

http://www.faxscape.com
http://www.netcentric.com
http://ntxc.com
http://faxsav.com/faxsavinternet
http://iquest.net/cgi-bin/vs

USING THE INTERNET TO SEND 'SNAIL MAIL'

You can use the Internet to save cash even if your contacts do not have a telephone, a fax, electronic mail or access to video phones. You can use the Internet to send them a letter via the ordinary postal service – **snail mail**. A number of companies – mostly in the USA at the moment, but also in Australia, for instance – provide a postal service for Internet users. All you do is send them an email message that you want as your letter. They print this out and send it via the local post service and charge your credit card. The benefit is that your letter gets to its international destination faster. Also, even with the handling charge, it works out cheaper than sending an international letter because the postage rate is local.

To find out more about sending ordinary letters via the Internet use your browser to go to the following URLs:

http://www.snailbox.com
http://www.outpost.net

USING THE INTERNET FOR INTERNAL COMMUNICATIONS

The Internet has led to a significant and dramatic rise in the speed with which businesses can communicate. However, there are two serious disadvantages:

- staff can be distracted by the wonders of the rest of the Internet

- even with security measures in place, confidential matters are still on a public network.

Both of these objections are answered with the use of an **Intranet**. An Intranet works in exactly the same way as the Internet, except it is private. It exists only on your company's computers and cannot be accessed by outsiders. You use web browsers in the same way, send electronic mail and take part in video conferences, all using the same technology. The only difference is that your Intranet is restricted to your company only.

Advantages of the Intranet

This has significant advantages:

- security is increased and confidentiality is maintained

- staff have fewer distractions available to them on the system

- speed of access is increased as there are fewer users

- you can still access the full Internet using hot links, widening the scope of your own system.

It is well worth investigating establishing an Intranet. It boost business communication for many firms and provides companies with excellent methods of updating staff. You can also provide on-line stationery banks with 'form' letters; you can have a question and answer forum with the human resources department; you can swop data easily; and you could even have a 'virtual' canteen or rest room where staff discuss the latest gossip! Establishing an Intranet is a highly logical step for many businesses, particularly those with more than one site.

If you want to establish an Intranet, get an expert in to help. You will need special hardware and software. You will also need an Intranet administrator to work full time on running the system.

CHECKLIST

1. The Internet is a highly valuable way of improving business communications by saving time and money.

2.   Once you have electronic mail be sure to establish a policy for its use.

3.   Consider expanding the scope of your electronic communications using telephone, fax, video and ordinary postal systems on the Internet.

4.   Establishing an Intranet is a logical step for many companies with more than one site. It helps reduce the problems caused by internal communication on the Internet itself, without losing any of the network's advantages.

CASE STUDIES

Family comes together thanks to the Internet

Darren works for an international manufacturing business. His career is doing well and he was recently given a posting to a new job in Malaysia. His home is in England and after much discussion he and his wife decided that they should not move together. The children were at a crucial time in their schooling and taking them away to another country would be damaging, Darren thought. Instead, Darren would work away from home, returning for the occasional weekend and spending all his holidays back in England.

The separation from the family would be difficult, but the posting was only for a year, after which he would return to the UK. The Internet, however, has helped the whole family cope with the separation. Electronic mail messages pass between Darren's computer in Malaysia and the one at his UK home almost every day. At weekends they have a family video conference call – it's a bit shaky but at least they can all see each other. The result has been improved happiness for the whole family without the need for expensive long distance calls.

Intranet rescues private bank

A private bank based in Germany was using the Internet to help its offices around the world. The bank stored important files on its home pages and staff around the world could call these up and use them when necessary. The files were contracts, standard letters and so on. There was no customer information. The Web page the bank designed also needed a password to access it, limiting the availability of the information to staff only. However, the password system was not the best devised and competitors soon were able to get copies of the contract files and standard letters.

The bank had to close down its Internet pages, but that slowed down productivity around the various branches. One of the customers was a computer consultant who suggested the problem could be overcome with an Intranet. The bank was able to establish its own system, using the same web pages it had previously published. The result was improved productivity, without the security problems.

DISCUSSION POINTS

1. What key strategies does your company need to establish for its electronic mail system?

2. Which additional Internet communications systems could your company use?

3. What is your company's communication policy? Can Internet communications systems help with this policy?

6
Obtaining Supplies from the Internet

If you are setting your business up to sell products and services on the Internet, you can be sure that other companies have done the same. That means you can buy almost every supply for your business through the Internet. Whether you want paper clips or a new executive car, you can get it through the Internet. The key reason why you might want to buy over the Internet is the convenience with which you can obtain supplies at competitive prices from a vast range of suppliers – more than you could visit in your home town.

THINKING ABOUT THE PROS AND CONS

Buying your supplies through the Internet has some advantages and some disadvantages. It also has consequences for the way you organise and manage your business.

Advantages
These include:

- instant access to wide variety of products and services

- availability of most up to date price lists

- reduction in search time for suitable suppliers

- flexible methods of payment.

Disadvantages
These include:

- not every type of supply is available over the Internet at the moment

- many suppliers are overseas, delaying delivery times to you

- centralised purchasing departments can lose control with company-wide access to Web pages

- the plethora of alternatives can waste time as you look for differences between suppliers.

DECIDING WHAT TO BUY FROM THE INTERNET

Although you can buy most things from the Internet, not every business need will be satisfied. General business merchandise, such as stationery, office equipment, computers and software, can all be purchased with ease over the Internet. But specific manufacturing machinery, for instance, is much less likely to be sold over the Net, though you will find marketing pages from potential suppliers.

To help you decide what you could buy from the Internet complete the following table below.

	Weekly	*Monthly*	*Annually*
Used by all staff			
Used by most staff			
Used by some staff			
Used by only a few			

Enter the details in this table of each of the products and services, together with their frequency of use. This will give you an idea of the supplies you need to buy regularly and those you only need occasionally. It will also show which supplies are most important to have in stock – those used by most staff every week.

When to buy locally

Items that are very important and which are used weekly are not always the best to buy from the Internet. This is because most suppliers on the Internet are international; there will be an inevitable delay in receiving such supplies because of the time needed to ship them to you. Increasingly you will find more local suppliers who can provide rapid delivery. However, for most day to day office supplies using a local high street supplier is probably the best thing to do – that is until the Internet increases its worldwide coverage, so you won't have to wait too long.

For items that you can hold in stock – some stationery materials, raw materials for manufacture and so on – or for long term purchases, like office equipment and computers, the Internet is already a viable source of suppliers.

Checking for availability

Once you have decided which products your company can purchase over the Internet you should search for suitable suppliers. Divide your potential purchases up into specific categories – such as paper, stationery items, printed supplies – also list any specific supplies peculiar to your business. This will increase your ability to search accurately on the Net and will save you time and phone call charges.

Once you have your list together call up the Internet and use the search engines to locate Web pages that meet your criteria. At this stage do not jump all around the Internet, going from one found page to another. Instead, save all the found lists you get, disconnect from the Internet and print out your search results. You can then read through them and sort out which pages will be of most use to you. Only then should you reconnect to the Internet to open up these pages. This method save you considerable time and call charges.

USING INTERNET SHOPPING MALLS

There are a number of 'virtual' shops on the Internet, sometimes called **malls**. These are areas of the Net where companies can buy space and have their products and services listed alongside a whole host of other retailers. These virtual malls are something like a covered shopping precinct, an indoor multiple store or a traditional shopping centre. They provide an area for shoppers to look at a whole range of suppliers, without having to search around the Internet.

These malls are useful as a starting point for your supply hunt. But don't rely on them. Good suppliers exist throughout the Internet and the shopping malls represent only a small proportion of your potential suppliers. It is best to rely on your own searches – which should produce those people who have their Net presence in malls anyway. If you only look at the shopping malls, you will inevitably miss some suppliers who could be better for your business.

Even so, some useful starting points for your shopping activities are the following URLs:

http://www.opse.com/mallistings
http://www.interpac.net/village
http://www.ukshops.co.uk:8000/welcome.html
http://www.yahoo.com/Business_and_Economy/Companies/ Shopping_Centres/Online_Malls/Regional

The URLs will open up sites of interest to anyone wanting to buy anything over the Internet and will also point you towards shopping centres throughout the world. However, they are only a small selection. At the end of 1996 there were over 800 virtual malls on the Net, representing thousands of shops. That's in addition to the thousands and thousands of Web pages offering items for sale. All the more reason then to make your searches for supplies highly specific.

CHECKING OUT SUITABLE SUPPLIERS

Once you have looked over the Web pages of your potential suppliers you will be able to start making comparisons and sort out the most likely candidates. However, how can you be sure that your chosen suppliers are as good as they say they are? And with many suppliers being thousands of miles away, how can you check them out?

Emailing other potential customers

Thankfully, the Internet does have ways in which you can do this. Firstly, you can email other potential customers to see if they have any experience of your chosen suppliers. You can also use the newsgroup system to post questions to particularly relevant groups. You can have answers emailed to your own mailbox. You could question people on the speed with which orders are handled, for instance, or how errors are dealt with.

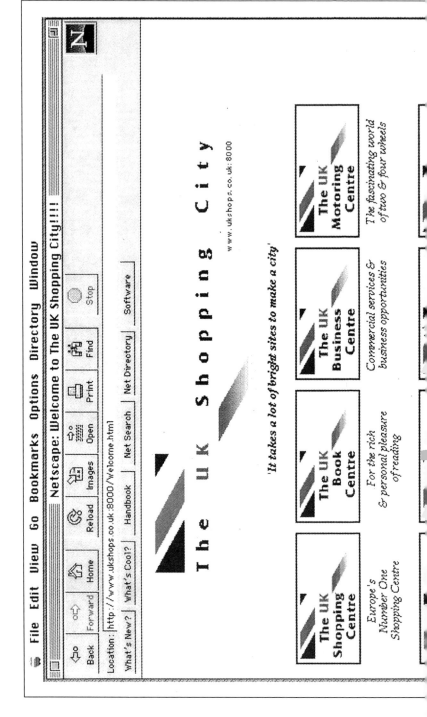

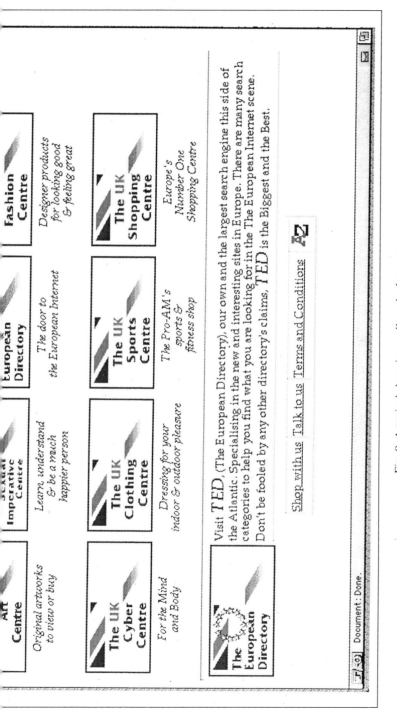

Fig. 9. A typical shopping mall on the Internet.

You can also use the Internet to find out information on potential suppliers. There is a variety of company information sites where you can find out published accounts, company profiles and so on. There are also places where you can discover what people are saying about Internet shops. One useful site is:

```
http://www.ewatch.com
```

This provides monthly reports on companies selling their wares over the Internet. Together with traditional company searches and information from other customers via newsgroups and email you should be able to select the best possible suppliers for your needs.

PLACING ORDERS WITH INTERNET SUPPLIERS

Once you have found suitable suppliers and decided which products to buy you can place your orders. Most Internet shops have an on-line order form: you simple enter the details of your purchases, provide payment, give delivery instructions and then await your goods. You may need to open an account with a supplier. Some companies, for your own peace of mind, ask you to open up an account through the postal service or with a telephone call. You provide credit card details and in return are given an account number. You then use this number in your Internet transactions. Because all activities on the Internet are traceable, it is obvious if someone else has attempted to use your account number.

Other companies simply ask for payment using credit cards; for this reason you may need to acquire a credit card that is used just for business or company purchases. All of the leading credit card companies provide such cards.

Using 'cash'

Alternatively, you may need to open up a **digital cash** account. This is whereby you exchange digital 'vouchers' in exchange for the goods and services you buy over the Internet. This is an increasingly popular way of performing Internet transactions. The company providing the goods will allow you to purchase the digital cash vouchers according to your needs. Essentially, digital cash is the same as opening up a credit account with a supplier. As you buy goods or services, your available credit reduces.

Obtaining proper receipts

Although most suppliers on the Internet provide delivery notes and receipts with your orders, some do not. Instead, they send you an email message which is your itemised receipt. You will need to print out this receipt and process it through your accounts in the normal way. Otherwise you may not be able to claim certain supplies against tax.

It is also worthwhile remembering that even though suppliers look cost effective, this may not be the case. In some parts of the world where sales taxes apply, or value added tax in Europe, businesses can benefit by reclaiming the tax portion of the costs. This provides a double benefit: the reclaimed tax makes purchases cheaper and the additional money can be invested before any proportion needs repaying to the national tax authorities. However, many Internet suppliers fall outside such arrangements because they are making their supplies from another country. They may charge you a sales tax, which you cannot reclaim being outside their legal boundary. Equally, they may not charge a value added tax, reducing your ability to benefit from the VAT system in Europe.

Check your receipts carefully. If your suppliers do not give you receipts send an email message with your suggested receipt details on it. Ask them to respond with a message saying 'agreed'. Your email pro forma receipt will be re-quoted in their message. When you print this out you will have an appropriate receipt for your accounts department.

Organising your business for buying over the Internet

Because the Internet is so widely available, almost anyone within your business can make purchases. Prior to using the Internet few people in the office would have known which company provided your stationery, for instance. With the Internet it's much easier because you will almost certainly have 'bookmarked' your key suppliers' pages. That means many people in your office can easily access these pages. Even if they can't locate or use your bookmarks, they can find out the likely suppliers with a simple search; it doesn't take much time and it's fun! That means you must have a purchasing policy in place, otherwise supplies will be bought by anyone in the company and your costs will soon rise as productivity falls.

To be certain that you get the most out of Internet purchasing:

- ensure only one person is responsible for all purchases over the Internet

- have a credit card account that is used exclusively for Internet purchases (you can therefore get a single detailed breakdown of all Internet buying activity)

- make the most of Intranets with an internal supplies ordering system that goes through one central department.

Each company, of course, will require a different combination of these, and other, policies. However, if you do not have some kind of written policy about what and when your company can order over the Internet and how it does it, you will inevitably waste money.

CHECKLIST

1. Select your possible purchases with care; not all supplies are suitable for obtaining via the Internet, no matter what the selling companies may claim.

2. Choose your suppliers carefully and make as many checks as you can about their record of service.

3. Ensure you obtain proper receipts for everything you buy over the Internet, even if it is a print out of an email message.

CASE STUDIES

Intranet boosts car manufacturer

An internationally-based car manufacturer used to obtain its stationery supplies from a variety of companies around the world. Each national affiliate firm of the global manufacturer bought its stationery locally. However, this meant that discounts were not as great as if the company bought on an international basis for all its worldwide companies. So, using the firm's Intranet, the supplies department set up a special ordering system for stationery. Companies would make requests for stationery items through order forms on the Intranet. These forms were sent to the supplies department which collated them and sent large volume orders to a specialist supplier in Germany via the Internet. The German supplier then processed the order, sending each item of stationery to the appropriate national firm of the car maker.

The company benefited by having a more streamlined stationery system. This saved time and money, enabled larger discounts and also ensured consistent quality worldwide. It also meant that staff in each country who had spent much of their time in processing stationery orders and dealing with local suppliers could now be used on more productive activities.

Vitamin supplier obtains packaging at a price

A vitamin supplier in the UK decided to try and buy packaging materials through the Internet. The idea was that the entire business was being developed to be an Internet only company – selling and buying through the Net. A suitable packaging supplier was selected, from the USA, which was slightly cheaper than the previous, UK-based, supplier. However, the vitamin company forgot to ensure that proper invoices were received. By the time invoices were obtained it was too late to complete the accounts for the year. This meant the auditors had no way of checking that purchases were real, even though it was obvious a purchase had been made because packaging had been used. The auditors therefore had to deal with the accounts differently. The result for the company was additional auditing costs, which were higher than the savings obtained on the new packaging.

DISCUSSION POINTS

1. Which supplies would your company choose not to obtain from the Internet?

2. How would your company ensure that Internet ordering was not open to abuse?

3. What checks would you put in place to make sure you had proper invoices for Internet-purchased supplies?

7
Controlling Internet Usage

One major advantage of the Internet is also a significant disadvantage. You can become hooked on the dynamic nature of the system, going from one page to another, linking from one computer in Sydney instantaneously to another in Alaska. You can hop around the world in seconds, finding out things you never knew before. The journey can be exciting, exhilarating, fascinating, absorbing. That means it can be time consuming, all pervasive and costly. Unless your business takes some kind of control over the Internet, it will drag your business down, increase its costs, make it less, rather than more, productive and eventually seal your fate of extinction. The very technology that can save your business could also be its downfall.

USING THE INTERNET EFFICIENTLY

Throughout this book there have been various hints and tips about how to ensure that your staff are productive and effective when using the Internet. Essentially these tips boil down to the following:

- have a written plan for Internet usage – a guide that all staff must follow

- ensure your business considers when and how to use the Internet, so that costs are kept to a minimum

- put someone in charge of the Internet, so they can police the usage.

Providing you do have some kind of plan and you have someone in charge, you should face few difficulties. Indeed, it could improve your business. Having someone in charge of the Internet in your business means you will have a responsible person able to keep up to date with the technology, enabling your business to stay one step ahead of the competition.

Just think of the Internet as another business tool. You have someone in charge of your computer systems, your company vehicles, your human resource management and so on. The Internet is just such a business tool – it requires management if it is to be exploited to its full effect and bring advantages to your company. Leaving staff to look into the Net on their own, unguided and unmanaged, will mean that your business will flounder. The staff will become hooked and be distracted from their normal work. Your productivity will go down and your costs will go up. Manage the Internet and the reverse will be true.

However, there are other issues that need considering in your business management of the Internet. These include:

- security

- safety

- exploitation.

MAKING SURE YOU HAVE INTERNET SECURITY

One of the main worries that businesses have when using the Internet is that someone will be able to 'hack' into their computers and extract confidential data. The last thing you want, for instance, may be a competitor obtaining vital details about a product prior to its launch. Your investment could be wasted. With your computer connected to the outside world via the Internet, the theoretical risk of such industrial espionage is greatly increased.

The risk of security problems mainly occurs when your computer is permanently connected to the Internet: if your system is linked via a leased line and your own machine hosts an Internet site. Many larger businesses prefer this option. It avoids the need to involve access providers and retains considerable control – something you have to give up when you use the computers of an external agency.

However, having your own computers connected to the Internet means that anyone, from anywhere in the world, can connect to your system. You have no real control as to who connects and when they do it. Your site is available for the world to see – after all that's the main reason for establishing an Internet presence anyway.

Reducing the risk of hacking

However, you can reduce the risks of people hacking into your system and obtaining confidential data. The two key ways of doing this are:

- server isolation

- passwords.

File Edit View Message Go Options Window

Netscape: Timecast Times for December 11, 1996

| Get Mail | Delete | To: Mail | Re: Mail | Re: All | Forward | Previous | Next | Print | Stop |

Folder	Unread	Total
Inbox	4	170
Outbox	0	0
Sent Mail	0	12
Trash	0	0
Sent	0	8

Subject	Date
What's ne...	5/9/96 9:32 a.m
Test page ...	6/11/96 11:25 ...
Fax to Pro...	31/10/96 2:53 ...
Timecast...	24/10/96 1:18 ...
Timecast...	30/10/96 10:4...
Timecast ...	7/11/96 3:09 pm
Timecast ...	14/11/96 10:0...
Timecast ...	21/11/96 6:45 ...
Timecast ...	28/11/96 7:43 ...
Timecast ...	6/12/96 12:26 ...
Timecast ...	Thu 11:10 pm
Test	26/11/96 1:34 ...
Financial T...	19/11/96 1:12 ...
ZD Net Up...	6/9/96 10:10 a.m
ZD Net Up...	13/9/96 3:23 pm
FWD>War...	22/10/96 10:4...

Subject: Timecast Times for December 11, 1996
Date: Thu, 12 Dec 1996 15:10:37 -0800
From: tctimes@listserv.prognet.com (Timecast Times)
To: gjones@zoo.co.uk

96

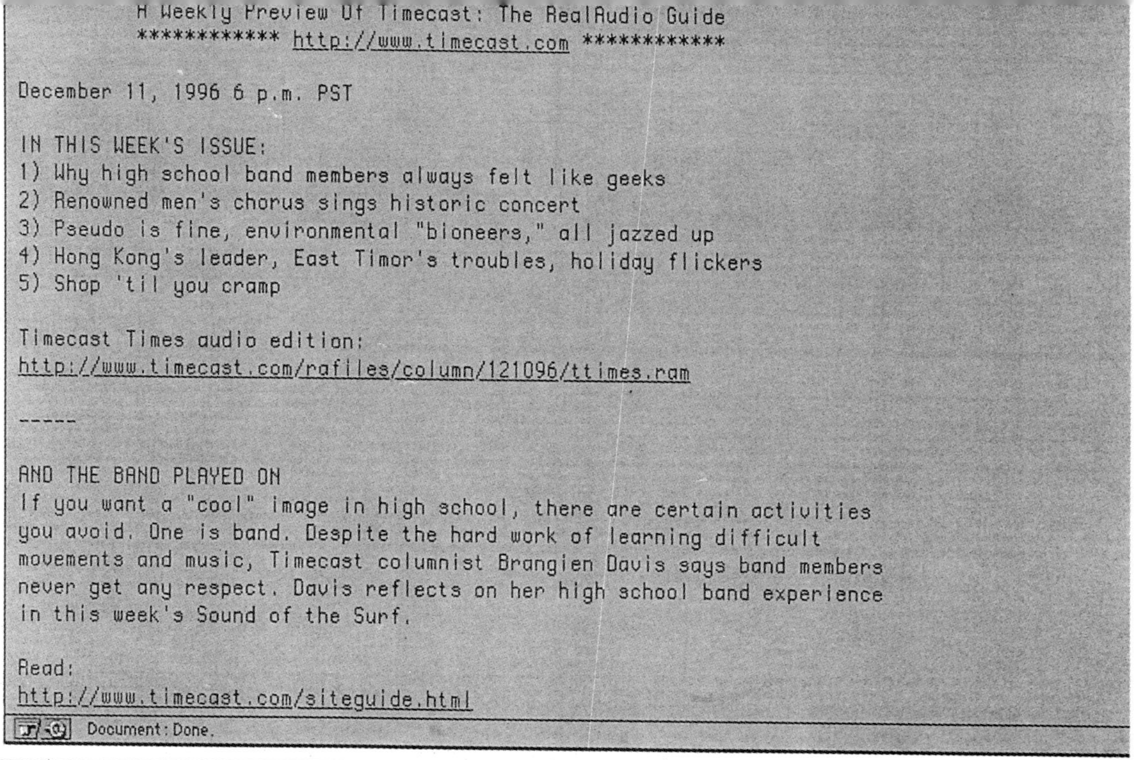

```
A Weekly Preview Of Timecast: The RealAudio Guide
************** http://www.timecast.com **************

December 11, 1996 6 p.m. PST

IN THIS WEEK'S ISSUE:
1) Why high school band members always felt like geeks
2) Renowned men's chorus sings historic concert
3) Pseudo is fine, environmental "bioneers," all jazzed up
4) Hong Kong's leader, East Timor's troubles, holiday flickers
5) Shop 'til you cramp

Timecast Times audio edition:
http://www.timecast.com/raffles/column/121096/ttimes.ram

-----

AND THE BAND PLAYED ON
If you want a "cool" image in high school, there are certain activities
you avoid. One is band. Despite the hard work of learning difficult
movements and music, Timecast columnist Brangien Davis says band members
never get any respect. Davis reflects on her high school band experience
in this week's Sound of the Surf.

Read:
http://www.timecast.com/siteguide.html
```

Document: Done.

Fig. 10. Keeping up to date with the news using the Internet.

97

Isolating your server

Your **server** is the computer you use to provide your Internet site. If this is your own machine it is best to make sure that it is not connected to other machines in your business. In other words, make your Internet server a stand alone, single computer. If your Internet manager needs to obtain data from your company network, use floppy disks or other portable storage methods like cartridges to transfer the data. Having your Internet machine linked permanently to your main network increases the risk of hacking. With the computer isolated, your main data is much more secure and cannot be accessed by outsiders. Only the data you allow on the Internet computer can be seen. Some people call this putting a 'firewall' around your system.

If you use an access provider's computer system you have effectively isolated your main computers anyway. Your pages only contain the material you send to the access provider, nothing else can reach the outside world and your own systems are secure.

Removing sensitive data

Some businesses, however, cannot have their main networks isolated from their Internet server. Say your company provides real time data, stock market prices, for instance. Updating your Internet computer without linking it to your main network would be impossible, if you wished to stay up to date and at least as far advanced as the competition. If this is the case you need to ensure that your computer network manager has isolated parts of the network that are not required for the Internet. In other words you need to take action to minimise the risk by removing data that you don't want the outside world to see.

For example, your network may include real time stock prices as well as your word processor and your customer database. If your Internet pages need to see the real time stock prices you need to move the word processing and database to another system. Essentially this means splitting the network, without changing the way your staff use their computer. This can be achieved with careful network planning. If you split your computer network you decrease the chances of breaches in security; if you allow your Internet machine to access the whole network, you increase the chances of hacking.

Using passwords

One way of reducing risks still further is to establish a password system. This means that only **authorised users** can access your pages. Two levels of passwords should be considered:

- internal

- external.

Internal passwords

With internal passwords you ensure that only authorised personnel can change your Internet system. This means that only specific members of staff can change your Web pages or adapt the system in any way. This avoids anyone with some kind of devious motivation, such as a grudge or malicious intent, from disrupting your system. Your password system should be confidential and people should memorise passwords and never write them down.

External passwords

External passwords protect your Internet pages from being viewed by just anyone. Your opening Web page could contain an application for a password to view or use other pages. Potential users of your system apply for a password and are notified by you via email if their application has been successful and what their password is.

Most companies provide passwords on payment of a fee. This enhances the service by enabling customers to view pages with greater detail than the general pages you provide.

Such a system of external passwords means you can control who uses your Internet pages. You know exactly who the people are, where they are from and their email address. Although such information is available for all Internet users, you have this information in advance, rather than in retrospect, providing you with greater security.

Using browser security measures

The Web browsers now also include a degree of security devices which mean that your system is more highly protected than before. However, these 'secure' transactions on the Internet are not completely secure: they can still be breached. Indeed, there are hackers who earn a living by keeping one step ahead of the security measures in the current range of browsers. So don't rely on browser security measures alone, even though they are significant and can provide you with considerable help.

ENSURING YOUR INTERNET SYSTEM IS SAFE

Security is one thing, but **safety** is another. Your Internet machine may be secure but is it safe from damage? It could be damaged through a

computer virus: a piece of computer code that can cause all sorts of problems. These codes are attached to other, innocuous, pieces of code, such as a program you download from the Net or data from a file you import. Once the virus is resident in your computer it can cause havoc. For instance, it may sit there, doing nothing until a particular date. Then it goes into action deleting all your data. Or it reproduces itself, attaching itself to each of your files, making them unusable. Or a virus might just display annoying, daft messages every now and then, doing no other harm. There is a complete virus industry and the Internet provides a highly suitable method of transferring viruses from one machine to another.

Avoiding virus infection

To avoid infection you must take the following measures:

1.   Have virus checking systems on all your computers.

2.   Have virus checking on your Internet usage.

3.   Have a written plan, that is put into action, for regular computer 'healthchecks'.

Every computer in your business should have virus checking programs. There are plenty of these around and, apart from minor differences, they are all excellent. If you don't use virus checking programs to protect your computer, you risk significant damage, even the end of your business.

Using Internet checking programs

Because viruses can be transmitted over the Internet with ease, you should have special Internet **virus checking** in place. These are special programs that can detect incoming viruses and warn you before they reach your machine. If the virus does get to your machine from the Internet, these programs can eliminate them before they do any damage. Once again, such programs are an almost vital requirement for Internet users.

Whatever method of virus checking you use, be sure to have some kind of regular healthcheck in place. Someone should be given the responsibility of checking your computers for hard disk problems and viruses at least once a month. When you use the Internet, computer health problems can be more likely, so get someone to make regular checks and your system should provide you with years of good service.

AVOIDING EXPLOITATION OF THE INTERNET

If you provide unlimited access to the Internet in your business it is bound to be exploited. It would be like providing every member of staff with a free car and free petrol, with no requirements to complete log books, claims for expenses or usage reports. Simply connecting your business to the Internet provides your staff with a heaven sent opportunity just waiting to be grasped.

With unlimited access they can get information on their hobbies,. have cheap phone calls with relatives who live abroad, download pornographic pictures, even watch a striptease. In fact, without control of some kind, your Internet business activities could become minor and the staff exploitation could become significant.

Controlling usage

You need controls using passwords, access times and so on, if your system is not to be exploited. As already explained, a written Internet policy is almost mandatory. An Internet manager is also a requirement to avoid exploitation. Make sure too that staff know that every visit they make to the Internet is logged and you know which sites they visit. For no other reason than the way the Internet works, your staff should be made aware that their every move on the Net is watched. That in itself should reduce the potential for exploitation.

However, for large businesses in particular, one of the key ways of avoiding exploitation is to establish an **Intranet**. An internal system that is clearly managed and well resourced will dramatically limit the potential for exploitation. But whatever way your business attempts to limit exploitation, don't avoid control. To do otherwise could spell ruin.

CHECKLIST

1. Ensure your business has a written Internet plan and code of practice.

2. Limit the ability of hackers to gain access to your confidential data.

3. Protect your systems from viruses.

4. Reduce the ability for staff to exploit Internet access.

CASE STUDIES

Accountancy firm loses money

A Bristol accountancy practice run by Steve employed ten staff altogether. His firm decided to use the Internet to provide services to international clients. They sent financial information via email and Steve's company sent back their completed books across the Net. At the same time, as added customer service, Steve searched the Net for useful information for each customer. This add-on service was designed to give Steve's firm a competitive advantage.

Steve couldn't understand why his computer and telephone costs had increased so dramatically once he joined the Internet. The access provider was local, so call charges shouldn't have risen so far. Only upon careful investigation did Steve discover that one of his book-keepers was using the Internet to gain information on flying – his hobby. Mike would spend great chunks of his time – at the end of each day – logging on to aviation sites, donwloading information about aircraft and sending email messages to other aviation hobbyists the world over. After discovery he was embarrassed and repentent. Foolish really, because Steve would have allowed Mike access to his favourite sites for specified amounts of time, had he asked. The problem was, Steve had not instituted an Internet plan and had not communicated anything to his staff, other than they could use the Net. That's why he lost money.

Mr Lum beats his competitors

Mr Lum runs a Singaporean car hire business. He uses the Internet to attract custom from international business people visiting Singapore. They order hire cars over the Net, arrange pick ups from the airport and book chauffeurs. One of Mr Lum's competitors also runs a similar system but, happily for Mr Lum, their business has suffered, following problems caused by the Internet. The competing firm allowed anyone to access their pages – no customer password was necessary. At first sight this seemed an advantage. However, it meant that a mean minded individual, who is still being tracked down, was able to transmit a damaging virus to them. This caused terrible problems that took weeks to resolve. Happily, Mr Lum has high levels of virus protection on his machine and can avoid such trouble, putting him well ahead of his competition.

DISCUSSION POINTS

1. How could your company ensure that staff do not exploit the Internet for their own use?

2. What methods of security could your company put in place to stop hacking?

3. To what extent are your computer systems safe from viruses?

8
Setting up an Internet-only Business

Although many companies can exploit the Internet and use it to improve existing business, the new technology is giving rise to businesses that couldn't have existed without the Internet. If your business is looking for new opportunities, or you are thinking of starting a unique business, the new technology of the Internet could be just the thing you are looking for.

Enhancing software support

Already there are businesses which have become established on the Internet which were not possible before, or which would have been prohibitively costly. Take, for instance, the software support business. Computer programs are updated almost every day. Ensuring that everyone in the world has the latest and most stable version is difficult. It costs money and this has to be charged to clients. This means some people avoid purchasing the latest update because of the costs. That in turn means such businesses fall behind. Later, when the software has been through a number of updates, the companies using old versions cannot obtain support and have to upgrade their entire systems at much greater cost.

Using the Internet, software manufacturers are able to make upgrades available over the Net. Companies are told about the upgrade via email and they can then log in and download the latest version all for the cost of a local phone call and a small handling charge. This encourages more people to upgrade, reduces the costs and ensures most people are using the latest versions. This, in turn, means more businesses are up to date and fewer companies suffer software related problems. Without the Internet, keeping everyone up to date and efficient would have been far too costly.

UNDERSTANDING AN INTERNET-ONLY BUSINESS

So your business could take on a new direction using the Internet, or you could establish an Internet-only business. Already many companies only operate via the Internet. Their services are marketed and sold only on the

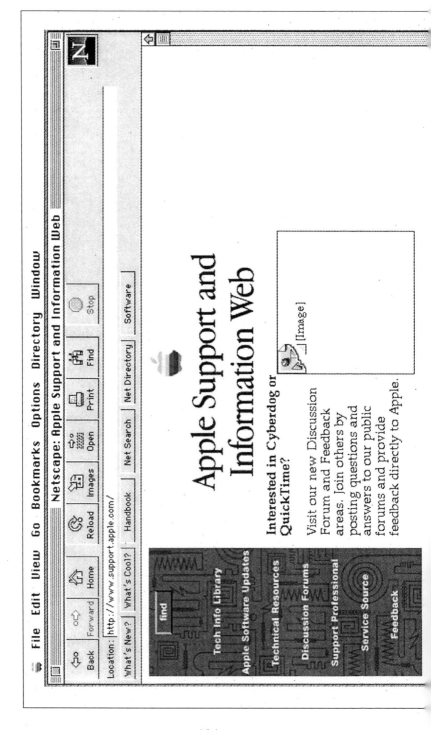

Apple is recommending that only customers with specific system software and Macintosh computers update their system with System 7.5.3 Revision 2. Visit the Apple Repair Extension Program.

Apple Tech Info Library

Access a subset of the same Technical Information Library (TIL). Apple engineers and technicians worldwide use to troubleshoot and solve your technical questions. With access to

Apple Software Updates Archive

Download the latest supported versions of Apple software, utilities, and updaters from our web based Apple Software Updates Archive or visit one of our public support resources to help you get answers for technical issues, find the software you need, get information on a particular product, find out who you can c Discussion Forums

The Discussion Forum area provides you with the opportunity to post your question or answers concerning Apple products to our public discussion areas. FAQ information will be updated as a re **Support Professional Program**

This award winning, fee-based support solution is the tool for corporate help desks, educational technology coordinators, or for anyone who supports Apple products and technologies. This section includes program options, pricing, **Service Source Online**

The official Apple Authorized Service Provider page designed to keep your local service provider up to date on the latest issues, and diagnostic troubleshooting techniques.

Cyberdog version 1.1!

Over 50,000 Items of information are stored at the www.Info.apple.com address.

Document : Done.

Fig. 11. One of the new breed of Internet businesses – software support.

Internet. Some business supplies companies, like stationery firms, only operate via the Internet. They have an on-line catalogue from which you select your purchases, which are sent using an on-line distribution supplier and your invoices are emailed to you. The on-line distributor can even keep you up to date on the progress of your order on special Web pages. Although suppliers could use traditional routes, the Internet provides them with a greater customer base and a competitive advantage.

Could your business be Internet-only?
So what kinds of business can become 'Internet only'? The kinds of firms that could use the Internet as a sole source of business include:

- accountants

- business writers

- information brokers

- insurance

- legal firms

- mail order retailers

- printers

- publishers

- software suppliers

- stockbrokers

- translation firms

- travel agencies.

For example, there are already translation companies that work exclusively on the Internet. You send your text for translation to the company, which forwards it to specialist translators who work on the Net. They send back the translation to the company, which sends the final material on to you together with an invoice. You settle this invoice over the Net using digital cash vouchers or a credit card. Such a system also speeds up the entire process, returning your translation much faster than using the postal service.

There are also travel agencies that work exclusively on the Internet. They provide hot links to pages of information about resorts and hotels. You make a booking over the Net, pay the bill using a credit card and receive an email confirmation.

Some printers also work exclusively on the Internet. You fill in a form with your print requirements and an instant price is calculated for you by the company's computer. You send your material to be printed across the Net, such as desktop publishing files, computer drawn logos and so on, together with full instructions. Your bill is emailed to you and you pay with a credit card or digital cash vouchers. Within a few days, your printed materials arrive on your doorstep.

As you can see, a whole host of services and products can be provided just using the Internet, without any other means of marketing or sales. Many businesses use the Internet only as an alternative outlet for their activities. However, some businesses are realising that the Internet provides more than another means of getting custom. They have realised that the Internet can provide a whole new way of working that is more efficient, more effective and better for customers.

WRITING AN INTERNET BUSINESS PLAN

If you think your business could be transformed by the Internet to become an Internet only business, you must write a plan. If you simply transfer all of your existing business to the Net, without carefully considering all the implications, you would soon be out of work. As with any kind of business activity, a full, in depth business plan will help you steer your course.

Planning for the future
Your Internet business plan should contain the following sections:

● your mission statement

● the advantages and disadvantages of using the Internet compared with other business systems

● the competition

● the customer potential

● your marketing plan

● your sales plan

- cash flows and profit forecasts

- future proofing plans.

Probably more important than anything else in an Internet business plan is the **future proofing** plan:

- How will your business survive as the technology changes?

- How will your company face up to more businesses exploiting the Internet?

If you are planning an Internet-only business these are vital areas you need to discuss and plan for. You will need to keep up to date on all areas of the Internet and ensure that your business stays one step ahead of the competition. The Internet is a fast moving world and if your business plan is static and inflexible, your business will collapse. In fact, you should review a plan for an Internet-only business at least four times each year. An Internet-only business is an exciting prospect for many people, but you must be able to keep up with the rapid pace of development.

CHECKLIST

1. Many businesses are suitable for establishing as or transferring to work on an Internet-only basis.

2. If you run an Internet-only business you need a well researched business plan that allows for future proofing as the Internet develops rapidly.

DISCUSSION POINTS

1. How well would your business transfer to Internet-only operation?

2. What aspects of your business would prevent you from running exclusively on the Internet?

3. How could you protect your business from future developments of the Internet that increased the competition?

Glossary

Access provider. This is the company (sometimes called a service provider) that sells you a method of connecting your computer to the rest of the Internet.

Archie. One of the methods of searching for files on the Internet.

Baud. The number of pieces of computer information transmitted per second by your modem.

BPS. Bits per second, transmitted by your modem.

Browser. A computer program that allows you to use the World Wide Web.

Client. The computer program you are using to do the particular work on the Internet you want.

Cyberspace. A term from a novel meaning the entire world of computers linked together.

Dial-up. Connecting to the Internet using your computer and a modem to make a call to your access provider.

Domain. A description of where a computer is somewhere in the world. The 'domain' identifies a particular part of the Internet.

Download. To transfer information to your computer from another one on the Internet.

Email. Mail sent electronically between two computers.

Email address. This is your address on the Internet. It is the specific pointer to you, just like your home address in the postal system.

Explorer. One of the most common browser programs.

FAQ. FAQ is simply shorthand for 'frequently asked questions'.

Firewall. The global term given to security systems used to prevent people accessing parts of your computer via the Internet.

Flame. To abuse people publicly on the Internet.

FTP. This is 'file transfer protocol', which is the way computers talk to each other to transfer information across the Internet.

Gopher. A searching system for finding things on the Internet.

Host. The computer your access company uses to connect you to the Internet.

Host name. The name given to the host computer.

HTML. The hypertext mark-up language used to create Web pages.

HTTP. This stands for 'hypertext transfer protocol'. Hypertext is a computerised method of improving the way you can use the system.

IP. This is the 'Internet Protocol'. This is an internationally agreed set of computer instructions that ensure that machines on the Internet can connect to each other and transfer information.

IRC. Internet Relay Chat – live discussions on the Internet.

ISDN. Integrated Services Digital Network (a fast telephone line system).

Leased line. A permanently open telephone line connecting a computer to the Internet.

Logging in. Entering your user details to let you access the system.

Mailbox. This is a storage area on your access provider's computer (host) in which information sent to your email address is stored.

Modem. A device that connects your computer to the telephone system and performs the necessary translation of the signals.

Mosaic. One of the common browser programs.

Netiquette. The standards of behaviour expected from Internet users.

Netscape. One of the most common browser programs.

Newsgroup. A specific area of the Internet for discussing a particular subject.

POP. This means 'point of presence' and indicates the locations where you can access the Internet from a particular access provider.

POP3. This has nothing to do with 'point of presence'. Instead this is a method for sending electronic mail messages. It stands for 'post office protocol number 3'.

Post. To send an email message or a message to a newsgroup.

PPP. This stands for 'point to point protocol' which is the way in which two computers at different sites talk to each other.

PSTN. PSTN stands for 'public switched telephone network' – the telephone system!

Server. A server is a large computer that is one of the main machines on the Internet.

Service provider. An access provider.

SLIP. This stands for 'serial line Internet protocol' and is one of the ways in which connected computers talk to each other.

Smiley. A facial expression produced by typewriter characters to indicate your mood to the recipient of your message.

TCP. This stands for 'transmission control protocol' and is the computer's program's method of communication with the Internet.

Telnet. A means of connecting directly to other computers on the Internet.

Upload. To transfer information from your computer to another one on the Internet.

URL. This is shorthand for an 'address', that is the location of the material you are looking for. URL stands for Uniform Resource Locator and it can be used to identify an individual computer, or a particular piece of information on a specific computer.

WWW. This stands for the World Wide Web, sometimes called W3, or more often the Web.

Further Reading

BOOKS

All You Need to Know about UK Internet Service Providers, Davey Winder (Future Publishing, 1995).

Guerrilla Marketing on the Internet, Jay Conrad Levinson and Charles Rubin (Piatkus, 1995).

How to Manage Computers at Work, Graham Jones (How To Books, 1993).

How to Use the Internet, Graham Jones (How To Books, 1996).

Internet Explorer Kit, Adam Engst and Bill Dickson (Hayden Books, 1994).

Internet Starter Kit, Adam G Engst (Hayden Books, 1994).

Launching a Business on the Web, David Cook and Deborah Sellers (Que Corporation, 1995).

New Rider's Official Internet Directory, Christine Maxwell (New Riders Publishing, 1994).

Paperless Publishing, Colin Haynes (Windcrest/McGraw-Hill, 1994).

Success with the Internet, Allen Wyatt (Jamsa Press, 1994).

Teach Yourself Web Publishing with HTML in a Week, Laura Lemay (SAMS Publishing, 1995).

The Internet Business Guide, Rosalind Resnick and Dave Taylor (SAMS Publishing, 1994).

The Internet Unleashed, Steven Bang (SAMS Publishing, 1994).

The Internet Yellow Pages, Harley Hahn (Osborne/McGraw-Hill, 1994).

The New Internet Business Book, Jill H Elsworth and Matthew V Ellsworth (Wiley and Sons, 1996).

The UK Internet Book, Sue Schofield (Addison Wesley, 1995).

MAGAZINES

All the computer magazines cover the Internet. All the specialist magazines are available from newsagents. The leading Internet magazines are:

.net
Internet
Net Guide
NetUser
What Net
Wired
Yahoo.

Net Guide, Wired and *Yahoo* are international magazines. All others are available internationally, though their supply may be more limited.

NEWSLETTERS

There are some international newsletters devoted to business on the Internet. These include the following:

Internet Business Analyst (Tel: +44 171 357 0842).
Internet for Business (Tel: +44 171 896 2234).
Internet Week (Tel: +01 301 424 3338).

Index

HOW TO USE THE INTERNET
A practical introduction for every computer user

Graham Jones

The fast-growing Internet is set to revolutionise personal and business communications across the globe, as well as entertainment, information and education. Unlike other books on 'The Net', here is a down to earth practical guide that will help you get the most out of this communication revolution. Gone are the heavy technical introductions, the in-depth computer instructions. Instead, here are simple, straightforward steps that anyone can use to get onto the Net and start exploring the new information super highway. Soon, nearly everyone in the developed world will have access to the Internet. This book shows you how and where to begin. Graham Jones is a leading business consultant and author. He is the author of *How to Manage Computers at Work* in this series, and has contributed to many computer magazines. He is Managing Director of a specialist business that utilises the Internet for up-to-date information.

126pp. illus. 1 85703 197 0.

FINDING A JOB IN COMPUTERS
How to share in the information technology revolution

Stephen Harding

Do you want a job in computers? Good, then this book is for you. Whether you are currently at school, college, university or simply contemplating a career change, this practical, step-by-step guide will show how to find that job. Dispelling the popular myth that experience and academic qualifications are prerequisites for many computing jobs, this book explains how and where new computing jobs are advertised, how to find the 90% of all computing job vacancies that are not advertised, how and where to get help and training, how to apply for computing jobs, how to secure and handle job interviews and how to ensure that employers have little choice other than to offer you the job. Steve Harding has over 15 years' experience of the computer industry. He is also the director of a successful software company.

183pp. illus. 1 85703 305 1.

HOW TO MANAGE COMPUTERS AT WORK
A step-by-step guide for beginners

Graham Jones

Here is a practical step-by-step guide which puts the business needs of the user first. It discusses why a computer may be needed, how to choose the right one and instal it properly; how to process letters and documents, manage accounts, and handle customer and other records and mailing lists. It also explains how to use computers for business presentations, and desktop publishing. If you feel you should be using a computer at work, but are not sure how to start, then this is definitely the book for you . . . and you won't need an electronics degree to start! 'Bags of information in a lingo we can all understand. I strongly recommend the book.' *Progress/NEBS Management Association.* Graham Jones has long experience of handling personal computers for small business management. The Managing Director of a desktop publishing company, he is also author of *How to Start a Business from Home* and *How to Publish a Newsletter* in this Series.

160pp. 1 85703 078 8.

HOW TO PREPARE A BUSINESS PLAN
Laying the right foundations for business success

Matthew Record

A business plan is the most important commercial document you will ever have to produce, whether you are just starting out in business, or are already trading. A well thought out and carefully structured plan will be crucial to the survival and longterm success of the enterprise. It will provide a detailed map of exactly where it is going, and help you forestall any problems long before they arise. A third of all new businesses fail in their first year, and of the rest a staggering 95 per cent will not make it beyond 5 years. Poor planning has been identified as the major cause of business failure. With the odds so stacked against success, make sure YOUR business gets off to the right start. Matthew Record is a business consultant specialising in the preparation of business plans for a variety of commercial clients. His company, Phoenix Business Plans, is based in Dorset.

158pp. illus. 1 85703 178 4.

How To Books provide practical help on a large range of topics. They are available through all good bookshops or can be ordered direct from the distributors. Just tick the titles you want and complete the form on the following page.

___ Apply to an Industrial Tribunal (£7.99)
___ Applying for a Job (£7.99)
___ Applying for a United States Visa (£15.99)
___ Be a Freelance Journalist (£8.99)
___ Be a Freelance Secretary (£8.99)
___ Be a Local Councillor (£8.99)
___ Be an Effective School Governor (£9.99)
___ Become a Freelance Sales Agent (£9.99)
___ Become an Au Pair (£8.99)
___ Buy & Run a Shop (£8.99)
___ Buy & Run a Small Hotel (£8.99)
___ Cash from your Computer (£9.99)
___ Career Planning for Women (£8.99)
___ Choosing a Nursing Home (£8.99)
___ Claim State Benefits (£9.99)
___ Communicate at Work (£7.99)
___ Conduct Staff Appraisals (£7.99)
___ Conducting Effective Interviews (£8.99)
___ Copyright & Law for Writers (£8.99)
___ Counsel People at Work (£7.99)
___ Creating a Twist in the Tale (£8.99)
___ Creative Writing (£9.99)
___ Critical Thinking for Students (£8.99)
___ Do Voluntary Work Abroad (£8.99)
___ Do Your Own Advertising (£8.99)
___ Do Your Own PR (£8.99)
___ Doing Business Abroad (£9.99)
___ Emigrate (£9.99)
___ Employ & Manage Staff (£8.99)
___ Find Temporary Work Abroad (£8.99)
___ Finding a Job in Canada (£9.99)
___ Finding a Job in Computers (£8.99)
___ Finding a Job in New Zealand (£9.99)
___ Finding a Job with a Future (£8.99)
___ Finding Work Overseas (£9.99)
___ Freelance DJ-ing (£8.99)
___ Get a Job Abroad (£10.99)
___ Get a Job in America (£9.99)
___ Get a Job in Australia (£9.99)
___ Get a Job in Europe (£9.99)
___ Get a Job in France (£9.99)
___ Get a Job in Germany (£9.99)
___ Get a Job in Hotels and Catering (£8.99)
___ Get a Job in Travel & Tourism (£8.99)
___ Get into Films & TV (£8.99)
___ Get into Radio (£8.99)
___ Get That Job (£6.99)
___ Getting your First Job (£8.99)
___ Going to University (£8.99)
___ Helping your Child to Read (£8.99)
___ Investing in People (£8.99)
___ Invest in Stocks & Shares (£8.99)

___ Keep Business Accounts (£7.99)
___ Know Your Rights at Work (£8.99)
___ Know Your Rights: Teachers (£6.99)
___ Live & Work in America (£9.99)
___ Live & Work in Australia (£12.99)
___ Live & Work in Germany (£9.99)
___ Live & Work in Greece (£9.99)
___ Live & Work in Italy (£8.99)
___ Live & Work in New Zealand (£9.99)
___ Live & Work in Portugal (£9.99)
___ Live & Work in Spain (£7.99)
___ Live & Work in the Gulf (£9.99)
___ Living & Working in Britain (£8.99)
___ Living & Working in China (£9.99)
___ Living & Working in Hong Kong (£10.99)
___ Living & Working in Israel (£10.99)
___ Living & Working in Japan (£8.99)
___ Living & Working in Saudi Arabia (£12.99)
___ Living & Working in the Netherlands (£9.99)
___ Lose Weight & Keep Fit (£6.99)
___ Make a Wedding Speech (£7.99)
___ Making a Complaint (£8.99)
___ Manage a Sales Team (£8.99)
___ Manage an Office (£8.99)
___ Manage Computers at Work (£8.99)
___ Manage People at Work (£8.99)
___ Manage Your Career (£8.99)
___ Managing Budgets & Cash Flows (£9.99)
___ Managing Meetings (£8.99)
___ Managing Your Personal Finances (£8.99)
___ Market Yourself (£8.99)
___ Master Book-Keeping (£8.99)
___ Mastering Business English (£8.99)
___ Master GCSE Accounts (£8.99)
___ Master Languages (£8.99)
___ Master Public Speaking (£8.99)
___ Obtaining Visas & Work Permits (£9.99)
___ Organising Effective Training (£9.99)
___ Pass Exams Without Anxiety (£7.99)
___ Pass That Interview (£6.99)
___ Plan a Wedding (£7.99)
___ Prepare a Business Plan (£8.99)
___ Publish a Book (£9.99)
___ Publish a Newsletter (£9.99)
___ Raise Funds & Sponsorship (£7.99)
___ Rent & Buy Property in France (£9.99)
___ Rent & Buy Property in Italy (£9.99)
___ Retire Abroad (£8.99)
___ Return to Work (£7.99)
___ Run a Local Campaign (£6.99)
___ Run a Voluntary Group (£8.99)
___ Sell Your Business (£9.99)

How To Books

___ Selling into Japan (£14.99)	___ Use the Internet (£9.99)
___ Setting up Home in Florida (£9.99)	___ Winning Consumer Competitions (£8.99)
___ Spend a Year Abroad (£8.99)	___ Winning Presentations (£8.99)
___ Start a Business from Home (£7.99)	___ Work from Home (£8.99)
___ Start a New Career (£6.99)	___ Work in an Office (£7.99)
___ Starting to Manage (£8.99)	___ Work in Retail (£8.99)
___ Starting to Write (£8.99)	___ Work with Dogs (£8.99)
___ Start Word Processing (£8.99)	___ Working Abroad (£14.99)
___ Start Your Own Business (£8.99)	___ Working as a Holiday Rep (£9.99)
___ Study Abroad (£8.99)	___ Working in Japan (£10.99)
___ Study & Learn (£7.99)	___ Working in Photography (£8.99)
___ Study & Live in Britain (£7.99)	___ Working in the Gulf (£10.99)
___ Studying at University (£8.99)	___ Working on Contract Worldwide (£9.99)
___ Studying for a Degree (£8.99)	___ Working on Cruise Ships (£9.99)
___ Successful Grandparenting (£8.99)	___ Write a CV that Works (£7.99)
___ Successful Mail Order Marketing (£9.99)	___ Write a Press Release (£9.99)
___ Successful Single Parenting (£8.99)	___ Write a Report (£8.99)
___ Survive at College (£4.99)	___ Write an Assignment (£8.99)
___ Survive Divorce (£8.99)	___ Write an Essay (£7.99)
___ Surviving Redundancy (£8.99)	___ Write & Sell Computer Software (£9.99)
___ Take Care of Your Heart (£5.99)	___ Write Business Letters (£8.99)
___ Taking in Students (£8.99)	___ Write for Publication (£8.99)
___ Taking on Staff (£8.99)	___ Write for Television (£8.99)
___ Taking Your A-Levels (£8.99)	___ Write Your Dissertation (£8.99)
___ Teach Abroad (£8.99)	___ Writing a Non Fiction Book (£8.99)
___ Teach Adults (£8.99)	___ Writing & Selling a Novel (£8.99)
___ Teaching Someone to Drive (£8.99)	___ Writing & Selling Short Stories (£8.99)
___ Travel Round the World (£8.99)	___ Writing Reviews (£8.99)
___ Use a Library (£6.99)	___ Your Own Business in Europe (£12.99)

To: Plymbridge Distributors Ltd, Plymbridge House, Estover Road, Plymouth PL6 7PZ.
Customer Services Tel: (01752) 202301. Fax: (01752) 202331.

Please send me copies of the titles I have indicated. Please add postage & packing
(UK £1, Europe including Eire, £2, World £3 airmail).

☐ I enclose cheque/PO payable to Plymbridge Distributors Ltd for £ [   ]

☐ Please charge to my ☐ MasterCard, ☐ Visa, ☐ AMEX card.

Account No. [   ]

Card Expiry Date [   ] [ ] 19   ☎ **Credit Card orders may be faxed or phoned.**

Customer Name (CAPITALS) ....

Address ....

.... Postcode...............

Telephone........................... Signature ....

Every effort will be made to despatch your copy as soon as possible but to avoid possible
disappointment please allow up to 21 days for despatch time (42 days if overseas). Prices
and availability are subject to change without notice.

Code BPA